D1518443

no coward soul is mine

EMILY BRONTË

poems

ODESSA
Rockledge, Florida
1993

Publisher's Cataloging in Publication
(Prepared by Quality Books Inc.)

Brontë, Emily, 1818-1848.
  [Poems. Selections]
  No coward soul is mine / poems by Emily Bronte.
  p. cm.
  ISBN 0-9634340-0-4 (library ed.)
  ISBN 0-9634340-1-2 (cloth)

  I. Title.

PR4172.A4 1993   821'.8
                                  QBI92-20336

no coward soul is mine

Emily Brontë
1818 - 1848

FOREWORD

There are a number of concerns to keep in mind when reading Emily Brontë's poetry: her youth, her secretiveness, her reclusivity, and her fierce independence that bordered on intransigence. Add to these an unparalleled imagination and the result is not only the most inimitable novel in the English language but also a small output of poetry, the best of which is comparable to any ever written.

The bulk of Brontë's surviving poems were written in her late teens and early-20's. After the publication of *The Poems of Acton, Curer, and Ellis Bell* (1846), which received meager but encouraging notice, she focused her creative energy on her great novel, *Wuthering Heights* (itself a towering poetic work). Brontë's early poems were devoted to themes and incidents of the mythical Gondal kingdom, a fanciful and epic joint creation with her younger sister Anne. By the time she was 24, her output slowed significantly, although she continually revised her previous efforts. Thus, her poetry is largely the work of youth, accounting for immature expression but also accounting for the unbridled energy. Youth reacts intemperately, emotes melodramatically, and is not dulled by extraneous trappings. All of these are hallmarks of the Gondal poems which are riddled with the rash acts of individuals who feel strongly but seldom think. We can speculate that as Brontë matured, so too her works. *Wuthering Heights*, although it maintains the intense passion of Brontë's poetry, is also a not-so romantic chronicle of household stewardship. In her mid-20's, Emily Brontë assumed the role of family manager. She had a bookkeeper's penchant for methodically recording mundane expenses and purchases, and she was also something of a financial speculator.

The much-repeated story of how Charlotte Brontë discovered her sister's poetry and Emily's bitter mourning of her exposure illustrates the mantle of secrecy she worked under. Although she shared some of her writings, not even her sisters knew the depth or breadth of her poetic mind. Writing in tiny script, stashing pages in a closely-guarded diary, Brontë could pour forth without fear of critical recrimination. But, although she was headstrong, she nevertheless was not immune to outsiders' opinions. We know, for instance, that in selecting and editing poems for publication she did make changes—often at Charlotte's insistence. In one last attempt at maintaining her privacy, however, she adamantly demanded the use of androgynous pseudonyms. Charlotte's story of gaining easier acceptance by publishers is after-the-fact rationalization; she squirmed uneasily when she unveiled the charade, fearing Emily's wrath for betraying their identities.

One of the puzzles of the Emily Brontë legacy is that her works are almost entirely creations of imagination, lying totally outside her own limited experiences. Besides the secretiveness, Brontë was a recluse. Her few periods away from home (amounting to three intervals totaling less than two years) were fraught with difficulty; away from Haworth she could not cope—Charlotte termed it "homesickness." But even in her own home she was withdrawn, preferring solitary walks and odd hours. The vision of her stalking the moors alone is not only appealing but accurate. She had no friends and few acquaintances, and was not troubled by the lack of either.

Genius, if not innately difficult in manifestation, is rarely suppliant. It requires a spirit independent of intellectual shackle as well as a certain stubbornness—traits Emily Brontë possessed in abundance. Although the daughter of the parson, she refused to teach Sunday School; her disdain for the medical profession may have cost her life. Only in her waning hours did she relent and accept, too late, a doctor's help. Charlotte's glossy remembrances, as well as the sketchy recollections of others, portray a woman determined to follow her own course, regardless of the consequences. A fragment found on a scrap of paper, written when Emily Brontë was in her mid-20's, sums up the essential honesty she lived and labored to reproduce in her works. That honesty—scrupulous, intense, passionate—is the bedrock of her poetry and the underpinning of her novel:

> Had there been falsehood in my breast,
> No thorns had marred my road,
> This spirit had not lost its rest,
> These tears had never flowed.

Strong I stand, though I have borne
Anger, hate, and bitter scorn;
Strong I stand, and laugh to see
How mankind hath fought with me.

Shade of mast'ry, I contemn
All the puny ways of men;
Free my heart, my spirit free;
Beckon, and I'll follow thee.

False and foolish mortal, know,
If you scorn the world's disdain,
Your mean soul is far below
Other worms, however vain.

Thing of Dust—with boundless pride,
Dare you take me for a guide?
With the humble I will be;
Haughty men are nought to me.

I'm happiest when most away
I can bear my soul from its home of clay
On a windy night when the moon is bright
And the eye can wander through worlds of light—

When I am not and none beside—
Nor earth nor sea nor cloudless sky—
But only spirit wandering wide
Through infinite immensity.

Love is like the wild rose-briar,
Friendship like the holly tree—
The holly is dark when the rose-briar blooms
But which will bloom most constantly?

The wild rose-briar is sweet in spring,
Its summer blossoms scent the air;
Yet wait till winter comes again
And who will call the wild-briar fair?

Then scorn the silly rose-wreath now
And deck thee with the holly's sheen,
That when December blights thy brow
He still may leave thy garland green.

Hope was but a timid friend;
She sat without the grated den,
Watching how my fate would tend,
Even as selfish-hearted men.

She was cruel in her fear;
Through the bars, one dreary day,
I looked out to see her there,
And she turned her face away!

Like a false guard, false watch keeping,
Still, in strife, she whispered peace;
She would sing while I was weeping;
If I listened, she would cease.

False she was, and unrelenting;
When my last joys strewed the ground,
Even Sorrow saw, repenting,
Those sad relics scattered round;

Hope—whose whisper would have given
Balm to all my frenzied pain—
Stretched her wings and soared to heaven;
Went—and ne'er returned again!

Mild the mist upon the hill,
Telling not of storms tomorrow;
No; the day has wept its fill,
Spent its store of silent sorrow.

Oh, I'm gone back to the days of youth,
I am a child once more;
And 'neath my father's sheltering roof,
And near the old hall door,

I watch this cloudy evening fall,
After a day of rain:
Blue mists, sweet mists of summer pall
The horizon's mountain-chain.

The damp stands in the long, green grass
As thick as morning's tears;
And dreamy scents of fragrance pass
That breathe of other years.

Well hast thou spoken—and yet not taught
A feeling strange or new;
Thou hast but roused a latent thought,
A cloud-closed beam of sunshine brought
To gleam in open view.

Deep down—concealed within my soul,
That light lies hid from men,
Yet glows unquenched—though shadows roll,
Its gentle ray cannot control—
About the sullen den.

Was I not vexed, in these gloomy ways
To walk alone so long?
Around me, wretches uttering praise,
Or howling o'er their hopeless days,
And each with Frenzy's tongue—

A Brotherhood of misery,
Their smiles as sad as sighs;
Whose madness daily maddened me,
Distorting into agony
The Bliss before my eyes.

So stood I, in Heaven's glorious sun
And in the glare of Hell
My spirit drank a mingled tone
Of seraph's song and demon's moan—
What my soul bore my soul alone
Within its self may tell.

Like a soft air above a sea
Tossed by the tempest's stir—
A thaw-wind melting quietly
The snowdrift on some wintery lea;
No: what sweet thing resembles thee,
My thoughtful Comforter?

And yet a little longer speak,
Calm this resentful mood,
And while the savage heart grows meek,
For other token do not seek,
But let the tear upon my cheek
Evince my gratitude.

Redbreast, early in the morning
Dank and cold and cloudy grey,
Wildly tender is thy music,
Chasing angry thought away.

My heart is not enraptured now,
My eyes are full of tears,
And constant sorrow on my brow
Has done the work of years.

It was not hope that wrecked at once
The spirit's calm in storm,
But a long life of solitude,
Hopes quenched and rising thoughts subdued,
A bleak November's calm.

What woke it then? A little child
Strayed from its father's cottage door,
And in the hour of moonlight wild
Laid lonely on the desert moor.

I heard it then, you heard it too,
And seraph sweet it sang to you;
But like the shriek of misery
That wild, wild music wailed to me.

On a sunny brae alone I lay
One summer afternoon;
It was the marriage-time of May
With her young lover, June

From her Mother's heart seemed loath to part
That queen of bridal charms,
But her Father smiled on the fairest child
He ever held in his arms.

The trees did wave their plumy crests,
The glad birds carolled clear;
And I, of all the wedding guests,
Was only sullen there.

There was not one but wished to shun
My aspect void of cheer;
The very grey rocks, looking on,
Asked, "What do you do here?"

And I could utter no reply:
In truth I did not know
Why I had brought a clouded eye
To greet the general glow.

So, resting on a heathy bank,
I took my heart to me;
And we together sadly sank
Into a reverie.

We thought, "When winter comes again,
Where will these bright things be?
All vanished, like a vision vain,
An unreal mockery!

"The birds that now so blithely sing,
Through deserts frozen dry,
Poor spectres of the perished Spring
In famished troops will fly.

"And why should we be glad at all?
The leaf is hardly green,
Before a token of its fall
Is on the surface seen."

Now whether it were really so
I never could be sure;
But as, in fit of peevish woe,
I stretched me on the moor,

A thousand thousand gleaming fires
Seemed kindling in the air;
A thousand thousand silvery lyres
Resounded far and near:

Methought the very breath I breathed
Was full of sparks divine,
And all my heather-couch was wreathed
By that celestial shine.

And, while the wide earth echoing rung
To that strange minstrelsy,
The little glittering spirits sung,
Or seemed to sing, to me:

"O mortal, mortal, let them die;
Let Time and Tears destroy,
That we may overflow the sky
With universal joy.

"Let Grief distract the sufferer's breast,
And night obscure his way;
They hasten him to endless rest,
And everlasting day.

"To Thee the world is like a tomb,
A desert's naked shore;
To us, in unimagined bloom,
It brightens more and more.

"And could we lift the veil and give
One brief glimpse to thine eye
Thou would'st rejoice for those that live,
Because they live to die."

The music ceased—the noonday Dream
Like dream of night withdrew,
But Fancy still will sometimes deem
Her fond creation true.

O Dream, where art thou now?
Long years have past away
Since last from off thine angel brow
I saw the light decay.

Alas, alas for me
Thou were not so bright and fair,
I could not think thy memory
Would yield me naught but care!

The sunbeam and the storm,
The summer eve divine,
The silent night of solemn calm,
The full moon's cloudless shine,

Were once entwined with thee.
But now with weary pain,
Lost vision! 'tis enough for me—
Thou canst not shine again.

In summer's mellow midnight,
A cloudless moon shone through
Our open parlour window
And rose trees wet with dew.

I sat in silent musing,
The soft wind wave my hair:
It told me Heaven was glorious,
And sleeping Earth was fair.

I needed not its breathing
To bring such thoughts to me,
But still it whispered lowly,
"How dark the woods will be!

"The thick leaves in my murmur
Are rustling like a dream,
And all their myriad voices
Instinct with spirit seem."

I said, "Go, gentle singer,
Thy wooing voice is kind,
But do not think its music
Has power to reach my mind.

"Play with the scented flower,
The young tree's supple bough,
And leave my human feelings
In their own course to flow."

The wanderer would not leave me;
Its kiss grew warmer still—
"O come," it sighed so sweetly,
"I'll win thee 'gainst thy will.

"Have we not been from childhood friends?
Have I not loved thee long?
As long as thou hast loved the night
Whose silence wakes my song.

"And when thy heart is laid at rest
Beneath the church-yard stone,
I shall have time enough to mourn
And thou to be alone."

The soft unclouded blue of air,
The earth as golden-green and fair
And bright as Eden's used to be:
That air and earth have rested me.

Laid on the grass I lapsed away,
Sank back again to childhood's day;
All harsh thoughts perished, memory mild
Subdued both grief and passion wild.

But did the sunshine even now
That bathed his stern and swarthy brow,
Oh, did it wake—I long to know—
One whisper, one sweet dream in him,
One lingering joy that years ago
Had faded—lost in distance dim?

That iron man was born like me,
And he was once an ardent boy:
He must have felt, in infancy,
The glory of a summer sky.

Though storms untold his mind have tossed,
He cannot utterly have lost
Remembrance of his early home—
So lost that not a gleam may come;

No vision of his mother's face
When she so fondly would set free
Her darling child from her embrace
To roam till eve at liberty:

Nor of his haunts, nor of the flowers
His tiny hand would grateful bear
Returning from the darkening bowers,
To weave into her glossy hair.

I saw the light breeze kiss his cheek,
His fingers 'mid the roses twined;
I watched to mark one transient streak
Of pensive softness shade his mind.

The open window showed around
A glowing park and glorious sky,
And thick woods swelling with the sound
Of Nature's mingled harmony.

Silent he sat. That stormy breast
At length, I said, has deigned to rest;
At length above that spirit flows
The waveless ocean of repose.

Let me draw near: 'twill soothe to view
His dark eyes dimmed with holy dew;
Remorse even now may wake within,
And half unchain his soul from sin.

Perhaps this is the destined hour
When hell shall lose its fatal power
And heaven itself shall bend above
To hail the soul redeemed by love.

Unmarked I gazed; my idle thought
Passed with the ray whose shine it caught;
One glance revealed how little care
He felt for all the beauty there.

Oh, crime can make the heart grow old
Sooner than years of wearing woe;
Can turn the warmest bosom cold
As winter wind or polar snow

Loud without the wind was roaring
Through the waned autumnal sky;
Drenching wet, the cold rain pouring
Spoke of stormy winters nigh.

All too like that dreary eve
Sighed within repining grief;
Sighed at first, but sighed not long—
Sweet—How softly sweet it came!
Wild words of an ancient song,
Undefined, without a name.

"It was spring, for the skylark was singing."
Those words, they awakened a spell—
They unlocked a deep fountain whose springing
Not Absence nor Distance can quell.

In the gloom of a cloudy November
They uttered the music of May;
They kindled the perishing ember
Into fervor that could not decay.

Awaken on all my dear moorlands
The wind in its glory and pride!
O call me from valleys and highlands
To walk by the hill-river's side!

It is swelled with first snowy weather;
The rocks they are icy and hoar;
And darker waves round the long heather
And the fern leaves are sunny no more.

There are no yellow-stars on the mountain,
The bluebells have long died away
From the brink of the moss-bedded fountain,
From the side of the wintery brae—

But lovelier than cornfields all waving
In emerald and scarlet and gold
Are the slopes where the northwind is raving,
And the glens where I wandered of old.

"It was morning; the bright sun was beaming."
How sweetly that brought back to me
The time when not labour nor dreaming
Broke the sleep of the happy and free.

But blithely we rose as the dusk heaven
Was melting to amber and blue;
And swift were the wings to our feet given
While we traversed the meadows of dew,

For the moors, for the moors where the short grass
Like velvet beneath us should lie!
For the moors, for the moors where each high pass
Rose sunny against the clear sky!

For the moors where the linnet was trilling
Its song on the old granite stone;
Where the lark—the wild skylark was filling
Every breast with delight like its own.

What language can utter the feeling
That rose when, in exile afar,
On the brow of a lonely hill kneeling
I saw the brown heath growing there.

It was scattered and stunted, and told me
That soon even that would be gone;
Its whispered: "The grim walls enfold me;
I have bloomed in my last summer's sun."

But not the loved music whose waking
Makes the soul of the Swiss die away
Has a spell more adored and heart-breaking
Than in its half-blighted bells lay.

The spirit that bent 'neath its power,
How it longed, how it burned to be free!
If I could have wept in that hour
Those tears had been heaven to me.

Well, well, the sad minutes are moving
Though loaded with trouble and pain;
And sometime the loved and the loving
Shall meet on the mountains again.

There was a time when my cheek burned
To give such scornful fiends the lie;
Ungoverned nature madly spurned
The law that bade it not defy.
O in the days of ardent youth
I would have given my life for truth.

For truth, for right, for liberty,
I would have gladly, freely died;
And now I calmly hear and see
The vain man smile, the fool deride;
Though not because my heart is tame,
Though not for fear, though not for shame.

My soul still chafes at every tone
Of selfish and self-blinded error;
My breast still braves the world alone,
Steeled as it ever was to terror;
Only I know, however I frown,
The same world will go rolling on

If grief for grief can touch thee,
If answering woe for woe,
If any ruth can melt thee,
Come to me now!

I cannot be more lonely,
More drear I cannot be!
My worn heart throbs so wildly
'Twill break for thee.

And when the world despises,
When heaven repels my prayer,
Will not mine angel comfort?
Mine idol hear?

Yes, by the tears I've poured,
By all my hours of pain,
O I shall surely win thee,
Beloved, again!

Harp of wild and dream-like strain,
When I touch thy strings,
Why dost thou repeat again
Long-forgotten things?

Harp, in other earlier days,
I could sing to thee;
And not one of all my lays
Vexed my memory.

But now, if I awake a note
That gave me joy before,
Sounds of sorrow from thee float,
Changing evermore.

Yet, still steeped in memory's dyes,
They come sailing on,
Darkening all my summer skies,
Shutting out my sun

Far away is the land of rest,
Thousand miles are stretched between
Many a mountain's stormy crest,
Many a desert void of green.

Wasted, worn is the traveller;
Dark his heart and dim his eye;
Without hope or comforter,
Faltering, faint, and ready to die.

Often he looks to the ruthless sky,
Often he looks o'er his dreary road,
Often he wishes down to lie
And render up life's tiresome load.

But yet faint not, mournful man;
Leagues on leagues are left behind
Since your sunless course began;
Then go on to toil resigned.

If you still despair control,
Hush its whispers in your breast.
You shall reach the final goal,
You shall win the land of rest

That wind, I used to hear it swelling
With joy divinely deep;
You might have seen my hot tears welling,
But rapture made me weep.

I used to love on winter nights
To lie and dream alone
Of all the rare and real delights
My early years had known;

And oh, above the rest of those
That coming time should bear,
Like heaven's own glorious stars they rose
Still beaming bright and fair

O transient voyager of heaven!
O silent sign of winter skies!
What adverse wind thy sail has driven
To dungeons where a prisoner lies?

Methinks the hands that shut the sun
So sternly from this mourning brow
Might still their rebel task have done
And checked a thing so frail as thou.

They would have done it had they known
The talisman that dwelt in thee,
For all the suns that ever shone
Have never been so kind to me.

For many a week, and many a day,
My heart was weighed with sinking gloom,
When morning rose in mourning grey
And faintly lit my prison room;

But angel-like, when I awoke,
Thy silvery form so soft and fair,
Shining through darkness, sweetly spoke
Of cloudy skies and mountains bare—

The dearest to a mountaineer,
Who, all life long has loved the snow
That crowned her native summits drear
Better than greenest plains below.

And, voiceless, soulless messenger,
Thy presence waked a thrilling tone
That comforts me while thou art here
And will sustain when thou art gone.

I saw thee, child, one summer's day
Suddenly leave thy cheerful play,
And in the green grass, lowly lying,
I listened to thy mournful sighing.

I knew the wish that woke that wail;
I knew the source whence sprung those tears
You longed for fate to raise the veil
That darkened over coming years.

The anxious prayer was heard, and power
Was given me, in that silent hour,
To open to an infant's eye
The portals of futurity.

But, child of dust, the fragrant flowers,
The bright blue sky and velvet sod
Were strange conductors to the bowers
Thy daring footsteps must have trod.

I watched my time, and summer passed,
And Autumn waning fleeted by,
And doleful winter nights at last
In cloudy mourning darkened the sky.

And now I'm come: this evening fell
Not stormily, but stilly drear;
A sound sweeps o'er thee like a knell
To banish joy and welcome care;
A fluttering blast that shakes the leaves,
And whistles round the gloomy wall,
And lingering long lamenting grieves,
For 'tis the spectre's call.

He hears me: what a sudden start
Sent the blood icy to that heart;
He wakens, and how ghastly white
That face looks in the dim lamplight.

Those tiny hands in vain essay
To thrust the shadowy fiend away;
There is a horror on his brow,
An anguish in his bosom now;

A fearful anguish in his eyes
Fixed strainedly on the vacant air;
Heavily bursts in long-drawn sighs
His panting breath, enchained by fear.

Poor child, if spirits such as I
Could weep o'er human misery,
A tear might flow—aye, many a tear—
To see the road that lies before,
To see the sunshine disappear,
And hear the stormy waters roar,
Breaking upon a desolate shore,
Cut off from hope in early day,
From power and glory cut away.

But it is doomed, and morning's light
Must image forth the scowl of night,
And childhood's flower must waste its bloom
Beneath the shadow of the tomb.

And first an hour of mournful musing,
And then a gush of bitter tears,
And then a dreary calm diffusing
Its deadly mist o'er joys and cares;
And then a throb, and then a lightening,
And then a breathing from above,
And then a star in heaven brightening—
The star, the glorious star of love.

The night is darkening round me,
The wild winds coldly blow;
But a tyrant spell has bound me
And I cannot, cannot go.

The giant trees are bending
Their bare boughs weighed with snow,
And the storm is fast descending
And yet I cannot go.

Clouds beyond clouds above me,
Wastes beyond wastes below;
But nothing drear can move me;
I will not, cannot go

All day I've toiled, but not with pain,
In learning's golden mine;
And now at eventide again
The moonbeams softly shine.

There is no snow upon the ground,
No frost on wind or wave;
The south wind blew with gentlest sound
And broke their icy grave.

'Tis sweet to wander here at night
To watch the winter die,
With heart as summer sunshine light
And warm as summer sky.

O may I never lose the peace
That lulls me gently now,
Though time should change my youthful face,
And years should shade my brow!

True to myself, and true to all,
May I be healthful still,
And turn away from passion's call,
And curb my own wild will.

How beautiful the Earth is still
To thee—how full of Happiness;
How little fraught with real ill
Or unreal phantoms of distress;

How Spring can bring thee glory yet
And Summer win thee to forget
December's sullen time!
Why dost thou hold the treasure fast
Of youth's delight, when youth is past
And thou art near thy prime?

When those who were thy own compeers,
Equals in fortune and in years,
Have seen their morning melt in tears,
To clouded, smileless day;
Blest, if they died untried and young
Before their hearts went wandering wrong,
Poor slaves, subdued by passions strong,
A weak and helpless prey!

"Because, I hoped while they enjoyed,
And by fulfillment, hope destroyed—
As children hope, with trustful breast,
I waited Bliss and cherished Rest.

"A thoughtful Spirit taught me soon
That we must long till life be done;
That every phase of earthly joy
Must always fade, and always cloy—

"This I foresaw, and would not chase
The fleeting treacheries,
But with firm foot and tranquil face
Held backward from the tempting race,
Gazed o'er the sands the waves efface
To the enduring seas—

"There cast my anchor of Desire
Deep in unknown Eternity;
Nor ever let my Spirit tire
With looking for What is to be.

"It is Hope's spell that glorifies
Like youth to my maturer eyes
All Nature's million mysteries—
The fearful and the fair—

"Hope soothes me in the griefs I know,
She lulls my pain for others' woe
And makes me strong to undergo
What I am born to bear.

"Glad comforter, will I not brave
Unawed the darkness of the grave?
Nay, smile to hear Death's billows rave,
Sustained, my guide, by thee?
The more unjust seems present fate
The more my spirit swells elate
Strong in thy strength, to anticipate
Rewarding Destiny!"

The evening passes fast away,
'Tis almost time to rest;
What thoughts have left the vanished day?
What feelings in thy breast?

*"The vanished day? It leaves a sense
Of labour hardly done;
Of little gained with vast expense—
A sense of grief alone!*

*"Time stands before the door of Death,
Upbraiding bitterly;
And Conscience, with exhaustless breath,
Pours black reproach on me:*

*"And though I've said that Conscience lies
And Time should Fate condemn;
Still, sad Repentance clouds my eyes
And makes me yield to them!"*

Then art thou glad to seek repose?
Art glad to leave the sea,
And anchor all thy weary woes
In calm Eternity?

Nothing regrets to see thee go—
Not one voice sobs, "Farewell";
And where thy heart has suffered so
Canst thou desire to dwell?

"Alas! the countless links are strong
That bind us to our clay;
The loving spirit lingers long,
And would not pass away—

"And rest is sweet, when laurelled fame
Will crown the soldier's crest;
But a brave heart with a tarnished name
Would rather fight than rest."

Well, thou hast fought for many a year,
Hast fought thy whole life through,
Hast humbled Falsehood, trampled Fear;
What is there left to do?

"'Tis true, this arm has hotly striven,
Has dared what few would dare;
Much have I done, and freely given,
But little learnt to bear!"

Look on the grave where thou must sleep,
Thy last and strongest foe;
'Twill be endurance not to weep
If that repose seem woe.

The long war closing in defeat——
Defeat serenely borne—
Thy midnight rest may still be sweet,
And break in glorious morn.

Far, far away is mirth withdrawn;
'Tis three long hours before the morn,
And I watch lonely, drearily:
So come, thou shade, commune with me.

Deserted one! thy corpse lies cold,
And mingled with a foreign mould.
Year after year the grass grows green
Above the dust where thou hast been.

I will not name thy blighted name,
Tarnished by unforgotten shame;
Though not because my bosom torn
Joins the mad world in all its scorn.

Thy phantom face is dark with woe;
Tears have left ghastly traces there:
Those ceaseless tears! I wish their flow
Could quench thy wild despair.

They deluge my heart like the rain
On cursed Gomorrah's howling plain;
Yet when I hear thy foes deride
I must cling closely to thy side.

Our mutual foes—they will not rest
From trampling on thy buried breast;
Glutting their hatred with the doom
They picture thine, beyond the tomb.

But God is not like human-kind;
Man cannot read the Almighty mind;
Vengeance will never torture thee,
Nor hunt thy soul eternally.

Then do not in this night of grief,
This time of overwhelming fear,
O do not think that God can leave,
Forget, forsake, refuse to hear!

What have I dreamt? He lies asleep
With whom my heart would vainly weep:
He rests, and I endure the woe
That left his spirit long ago.

I know not how it falls on me,
    This summer evening, hushed and lone;
Yet the faint wind comes soothingly
    With something of an olden tone.

Forgive me if I've shunned so long
    Your gentle greeting, earth and air!
But sorrow withers even the strong,
    And who can fight against despair?

A little while, a little while,
The noisy crowd is barred away;
And I can sing and I can smile
A little while I've holiday!

Where wilt thou go, my harassed heart?
Full many a land invites thee now;
And places near and far apart
Have rest for thee, my weary brow.

There is a spot 'mid barren hills
Where winter howls and driving rain,
But if the dreary tempest chills
There is a light that warms again.

The house is old, the trees are bare
And moon-less bends the misty dome,
But what on earth is half so dear,
So longed for, as the hearth of home?

The mute bird sitting on the stone,
The dank moss dripping from the wall,
The garden-walk with weeds o'ergrown,
I love them—how I love them all!

Shall I go there? or shall I seek
Another clime, another sky,
Where tongues familiar music speak
In accents dear to memory?

Yes, as I mused, the naked room
The flickering firelight died away
And from the midst of cheerless gloom
I passed to bright, unclouded day—

A little and a lone green lane
That opened on a common wide;
A distant, dreamy, dim blue chain
Of mountains circling every side;

A heaven so clear, an earth so calm,
So sweet, so soft, so hushed an air
And deepening still the dream-like charm,
Wild moor-sheep feeding everywhere—

That was the scene; I knew it well,
I knew the pathways far and near
That winding o'er each billowy swell
Marked out the tracks of wandering deer.

Could I have lingered but an hour
It well had paid a week of toil,
But truth has banished fancy's power;
I hear my dungeon bars recoil—

Even as I stood with raptured eye
Absorbed in bliss so deep and dear,
My hour of rest had fleeted by
And given me back to weary care.

O God of heaven! the dream of horror,
The frightful dream is over now;
The sickened heart, the blasting sorrow,
The ghastly night, ghastlier morrow,
The aching sense of utter woe;

The burning tears that would keep welling,
The groans that mocked at every tear
That burst from out their dreary dwelling
As if each gasp were life expelling,
But life was nourished by despair;

The tossing and the anguished pining;
The grinding teeth and staring eye;
The agony of still repining,
When not a spark of hope was shining
From gloomy fate's relentless sky;

The impatient rage, the useless shrinking
From thoughts that yet could not be borne;
The soul that was for ever thinking,
Till nature, maddened, tortured, sinking,
At last refused to mourn.

It's over now—and I am free,
And the ocean wind is caressing me,
The wild wind from that wavy main
I never thought to see again

Bless thee, Bright Sea—and glorious dome,
And my own world, my spirit's home;
Bless thee, Bless all—I cannot speak;
My voice is choked, but not with grief;
And salt drops from my haggard cheek
Descend, like rain upon the heath.

How long they've wet a dungeon floor,
Falling on flag-stones damp and grey!
I used to weep even in my sleep;
The night was dreadful, like the day.

I used to weep when winter's snow
Whirled through the grating stormily,
But then it was a calmer woe
For everything was drear as me.

The bitterest time, the worst of all,
Was that in which the summer sheen
Cast a green luster on the wall
That told of fields of lovelier green.

Often I've sat down on the ground,
Gazing up to that flush scarce seen
Till, heedless of the darkness round,
My soul has sought a land serene.

It sought the arch of heaven divine,
The pure blue heaven with clouds of gold;
It sought thy father's home and mine
As I remembered it of old.

O even now too horribly
Come back the feelings that would swell,
When with my face hid on my knee
I strove the bursting groans to quell.

I flung myself upon the stone,
I howled and tore my tangled hair,
And then, when the first gush had flown,
Lay in unspeakable despair.

Sometimes a curse, sometimes a prayer
Would quiver on my parched tongue;
But both without a murmur there
Died in the breast from whence they sprung.

And so the day would fade on high,
And darkness quench that lonely beam,
And slumber mould my misery
Into some strange and spectral dream
Whose phantom horrors made me know
The worst extent of human woe.

But this is past, and why return
O'er such a past to brood and mourn?
Shake off the fetters, break the chain,
And live and love and smile again.

The waste of youth, the waste of years,
Departed in that dungeon's thrall;
The gnawing grief, the hopeless tears,
Forget them — O forget them all.

There let thy bleeding branch atone
For every torturing tear:
Shall my young sins, my sins alone,
Be everlasting here?

Who bade thee keep that cursed name
A pledge for memory?
As if Oblivion ever came
To breathe its bliss on me;

As if, through all the 'wildering maze
Of mad hours left behind,
I once forgot the early days
That thou wouldst call to mind

High waving heather, 'neath stormy blasts bending,
Midnight and moonlight and bright shining stars;
Darkness and glory rejoicingly blending,
Earth rising to heaven and heaven descending,
Man's spirit away from its drear dungeon sending,
Bursting the fetters and breaking the bars.

All down the mountain sides, wild forests lending
One mighty voice to life-giving wind;
Rivers their banks in the jubilee rending,
Fast through the valleys a reckless course wending,
Wider and deeper their waters extending,
Leaving a desolate desert behind.

Shining and lowering and swelling and dying,
Changing forever from midnight to noon;
Roaring like thunder, like soft music sighing,
Shadows on shadows advancing and flying,
Lightning-bright flashes the deep gloom defying,
Coming as swiftly and fading as soon.

It is too late to call thee now:
I will not nurse that dream again;
For every joy that lit my brow
Would bring its after-storm of pain.

Besides, the mist is half withdrawn;
The barren mountain side lies bare;
And sunshine and awaking morn
Paint no more golden visions there.

Yet, ever in my grateful breast,
Thy darling shade shall cherished be;
For God alone doth know how blest
My early years have been in thee!

The night of storms has passed,
The sunshine bright and clear
Gives glory to the verdant waste
And warms the breezy air;

And I would leave my bed,
Its cheering smile to see,
To chase the visions from my head
Whose forms have troubled me.

In all the hours of gloom
My soul was wrapped away;
I dreamt I stood by a marble tomb
Where royal corpses lay.

It was just the time of eve,
When parted ghosts might come
Above their prisoned dust to grieve
And wail their woeful doom.

And truly at my side
I saw a shadowy thing
Most dim, and yet its presence there
Curdled my blood with ghastly fear
And ghastlier wondering.

My breath I could not draw,
The air so biting;
But still my eyes with maddening gaze
Were fixed upon its fearful face,
As its were fixed on me.

I fell down on the stone,
But could not turn away;
My words died in a voiceless moan
When I began to pray.

And still it bent above,
Its features full in view;
It seemed close by, and yet more far
Than this world from the farthest star
That tracks the boundless blue.

Indeed, 'twas not the space
Of earth or time between,
But the sea of death's eternity,
The gulf o'er which mortality
Has never, never been.

O bring not back again
The horror of that hour
When its lips opened, and a sound
Awoke the stillness reigning round,
Faint as a dream, but the earth shrank
And heaven's lights shivered 'neath its power.

I'll not weep that thou art going to leave me,
There's nothing lovely here;
And doubly will the dark world grieve me
While thy heart suffers there.

I'll not weep, because the summer's glory
Must always end in gloom;
And, follow out the happiest story—
It closes with a tomb!

And I am weary of the anguish
Increasing winters bear;
Weary to watch the spirit languish
Through years of dead despair.

So, if a tear, when thou art dying,
Should haply fall from me,
It is but that my soul is sighing
To go and rest with thee.

Month after month, year after year,
My harp has poured a dreary strain;
At length a livelier note shall cheer,
And pleasure tune its chords again.

What though the stars and fair moonlight
Are quenched in morning dull and grey?
They are but tokens of the night,
And this, my soul, is day.

Ah! why, because the dazzling sun
Restored our Earth to joy
Have you departed, every one,
And left a desert sky?

All through the night, your glorious eyes
Were gazing down in mine,
And with a full heart's thankful sighs
I blessed that watch divine!

I was at peace, and drank your beams
As they were life to me
And revelled in my changeful dreams
Like petrel on the sea.

Thought followed thought—star followed star
Through boundless regions on,
While one sweet influence, near and far,
Thrilled through and proved us one.

Why did the morning dawn to break
So great, so pure a spell,
And scorch with fire the tranquil cheek
Where your cool radiance fell?

Blood-red he rose, and arrow-straight
His fierce beams struck my brow:
The soul of Nature sprang elate,
But mine sank sad and low!

My lids closed down—yet through their veil
I saw him blazing still;
And steep in gold the misty dale,
And flash upon the hill.

I turned me to the pillow then
To call back Night, and see
Your worlds of solemn light, again
Throb with my heart and me!

It would not do—the pillow glowed
And glowed both roof and floor,
And birds sang loudly in the wood,
And fresh winds shook the door.

The curtains wave, the wakened flies
Were murmuring round my room,
Imprisoned there, till I should rise
And give them leave to roam.

O Stars and Dreams and Gentle Night;
O Night and Stars return!
And hide me from the hostile light
That does not warm, but burn—

That drains the blood of suffering men;
Drink tears, instead of dew;
Let me sleep through his blinding reign,
And only wake with you!

There should be no despair for you
While nightly stars are burning,
While evening pours it silent dew
And sunshine gilds the morning.

There should be no despair, though tears
May flow down like a river:
Are not the best beloved of years
Around your heart forever?

They weep—you weep—it must be so;
Winds sigh as you are sighing;
And Winter sheds its grief in snow
Where Autumn's leaves are lying.

Yet these revive, and from their fate
Your fate cannot be parted,
Then journey on, if not elate
Still, never broken-hearted!

Death, that struck when I was most confiding
In my certain Faith of Joy to be,
Strike again, Time's withered branch dividing
From the fresh root of Eternity!

Leaves, upon Time's branch, were growing brightly,
Full of sap and full of silver dew;
Birds, beneath its shelter, gathered nightly;
Daily, round its flowers, the wild bees flew.

Sorrow passed and plucked the golden blossom,
Guilt stripped off the foliage in its pride;
But, within its parent's kindly bosom,
Flowed forever Life's restoring tide.

Little mourned I for the parted Gladness,
For the vacant nest and silent song;
Hope was there and laughed me out of sadness,
Whispering, "Winter will not linger long."

And behold, with tenfold increase blessing
Spring adorned the beauty-burdened spray;
Wind and rain and fervent heat caressing
Lavished glory on that second May.

High it rose; no winged grief could sweep it;
Sin was scared to distance with its shine:
Love and its own life had power to keep it
From all wrong, from every blight but thine!

Cruel Death! The young leaves droop and languish!
Evening's gentle air may still restore—
No: the morning sunshine mocks my anguish—
Time for me must never blossom more!

Strike it down, that other boughs may flourish
Where that perished sapling used to be;
Thus, at least, its mouldering corpse will nourish
That from which it sprung—Eternity.

When weary with the long day's care,
And earthly change from pain to pain,
And lost, and ready to despair,
Thy kind voice calls me back again—
O my true friend, I am not lone
While thou canst speak with such a tone!

So hopeless is the world without,
The world within I doubly prize;
Thy world where guile and hate and doubt
And cold suspicion never rise;
Where thou and I and Liberty
Have undisputed sovereignty.

What matters it that all around
Danger, and guilt, and darkness lie,
If but within our bosom's bound
We hold a bright, untroubled sky,
Warm with ten thousand mingled rays
Of suns that know no winter days?

Reason indeed may oft complain
For Nature's sad reality,
And tell the suffering heart how vain
Its cherished dreams must always be;
And Truth may rudely trample down
The flowers of Fancy newly blown.

But thou art ever there to bring
The hovering vision back, and breathe
New glories o'er the blighted spring
And call a lovelier life from death,
And whisper with a voice divine
Of real worlds as bright as thine.

I trust not to thy phantom bliss,
Yet still in evening's quiet hour
With never-failing thankfulness
I welcome thee, benignant power,
Sure solacer of human cares
And sweeter hope, when hope despairs.

Fall, leaves, fall; die, flowers, away;
Lengthen night and shorten day;
Every leaf speaks bliss to me
Fluttering from the autumn tree.
I shall smile when wreaths of snow
Blossom where the rose should grow;
I shall sing when night's decay
Ushers in a drearier day

Shall Earth no more inspire thee,
Thou lonely dreamer now?
Since passion may not fire thee
Shall Nature cease to bow?

Thy mind is ever moving
In regions dark to thee;
Recall its useless roving—
Come back and dwell with me.

I know my mountain breezes
Enchant and soothe thee still—
I know my sunshine pleases
Despite thy wayward will.

When day with evening blending
Sinks from the summer sky,
I've seen thy spirit bending
In fond idolatry.

I've watched thee every hour;
I know my mighty sway,
I know my magic power
To drive thy griefs away.

Few hearts to mortals given
On earth so wildly pine;
Yet none would ask a Heaven
More like this Earth than thine.

Then let my winds caress thee;
Thy comrade let me be—
Since nought beside can bless thee,
Return and dwell with me.

The wind, I hear it sighing
With Autumn's saddest sound;
Withered leaves as thick are lying
As spring flowers on the ground.

This dark night has won me
To wander far away;
Old feelings gather fast upon me
Like vultures round their prey.

Kind were they once, and cherished,
But cold and cheerless now;
I would their lingering shades had perished
When their light left my brow.

'Tis like old age pretending
The softness of a child,
My altered, hardened spirit bending
To meet their fancies wild.

Yet could I with past pleasures
Past woe's oblivion buy,
That by the death of my dearest treasures
My deadliest pains might die,

O then another daybreak
Might hap'ly dawn above,
Another summer gild my cheek,
My soul, another love.

The day is done, the winter sun
Is setting in its sullen sky;
And drear the course that has been run,
And dim the beams that slowly die.

No star will light my coming night;
No moon of hope for me will shine;
I mourn not heaven would blast my sight,
And I never longed for ways divine.

Through Life's hard Task I did not ask
Celestial aid, celestial cheer;
I saw my fate without its mask,
And met it too without a tear.

The grief that pressed this living breast
Was heavier far than earth can be;
And who would dread eternal rest
When labour's hire was agony?

Dark falls the fear of this despair
On spirits born for happiness;
But I was bred the mate of care,
The foster-child of sore distress.

No sighs for me, no sympathy,
No wish to keep my soul below;
The heart is dead since infancy,
Unwept for-let the body go.

Fair sinks the summer evening now
In softened glory round my home;
The sky upon its holy brow
Wears not a cloud that speaks of gloom.

The old tower, shrined in golden light,
Looks down on the descending sun—
So gently evening blends with night,
You scarce can say that day is done.

And this is just the joyous hour
When we were wont to burst away,
To 'scape from labour's tyrant power
And cheerfully go out to play.

Then why is all so sad and lone?
No merry footstep on the stair—
No laugh—no heart-awaking tone,
But voiceless silence everywhere.

I've wandered round our garden ground,
And still it seemed, at every turn,
That I should greet approaching feet,
And words upon the breezes borne.

In vain—they will not come today,
And morning's beam will rise as drear;
Then tell me—are they gone for aye
Our sun blinks through the mists of care?

Ah no; reproving Hope doth say,
Departed joys 'tis fond to mourn,
When every storm that hides its ray
Prepares a more divine return.

I am the only being whose doom
No tongue would ask, no eye would mourn;
I never caused a thought of gloom,
A smile of joy, since I was born.

In secret pleasure, secret tears,
This changeful life has slipped away,
As friendless after eighteen years,
As lone as on my natal day.

There have been times I cannot hide,
There have been times when this was drear,
When my sad soul forgot its pride
And longed for one to love me here.

But those were in the early glow
Of feelings since subdued by care;
And they have died so long ago
I hardly now believe they were.

First melted off the hope of youth,
Then fancy's rainbow fast withdrew;
And then experience told me truth
In mortal bosoms never grew.

'Twas grief enough to think mankind
All hollow, servile, insincere;
But worse to trust to my own mind
And find the same corruption there.

Tell me, tell me, smiling child,
What the past is like to thee?
"An Autumn evening soft and mild
With a wind that sighs mournfully."

Tell me, what is the present hour?
"A green and flowery spray
Where a young bird sits gathering its power
To mount and fly away."

And what is the future, happy one?
"A sea beneath a cloudless sun;
A mighty, glorious, dazzling sea
Stretching into infinity."

Riches I hold in light esteem
And Love I laugh to scorn;
And lust of Fame was but a dream
That vanished with the morn—

And if I pray, the only prayer
That moves my lips for me
Is — "Leave the heart that now I bear
And give me liberty."

Yes, as my swift days near their goal
'Tis all that I implore—
In life and death a chainless soul
With courage to endure!

Methinks this heart should rest awhile,
So stilly round the evening falls;
The veiled sun sheds no parting smile,
Not mirth nor music wakes my halls.

I have sat lonely all the day
Watching the drizzly mist descend
And first conceal the hills in grey
And then along the valleys wend.

And I have sat and watched the trees
And the sad flowers—how drear they blow:
Those flowers were formed to feel the breeze
Wave their light leaves in summer's glow.

Yet their lives passed in gloomy woe
And hopeless comes its dark decline,
And I lament, because I know
That cold departure pictures mine.

"Enough of Thought, Philosopher;
Too long hast thou been dreaming
Unlightened, in this chamber drear
While summer's sun is beaming—
Space-sweeping soul, what sad refrain
Concludes thy musings once again?

"O for the time when I sleep
Without identity,
And never care how rain may steep
Or snow may cover me!

"No promised Heaven, these wild Desires
Could all or half fulfil;
No threatened Hell, with quenchless fires,
Subdue this quenchless will!"

—So said I, and still say the same;
—Still to my Death will say—
Three Gods within this little frame
Are warring night and day.

Heaven could not hold them all, and yet
They all are held in me
And must be mine till I forget
My present entity.

O for the time when in my breast
Their struggles will be o'er;
O for the day when I shall rest,
And never suffer more!

"I saw a Spirit standing, Man,
Where thou doest stand—an hour ago;
And round his feet, three rivers ran
Of equal depth and equal flow—

"A Golden stream, and one like blood,
And one like Sapphire, seemed to be,
But where they joined their triple flood
It tumbled in an inky sea.

"The Spirit sent his dazzling gaze
Down through that Ocean's gloomy night,
Then—kindling all with sudden blaze,
The glad deep sparkled wide and bright—
White as the sun; far, far more fair
Than its divided sources were!"

—And even for that Spirit, Seer,
I've watched and sought my lifetime long;
Sought Him in Heaven, Hell, Earth and Air,
An endless search—and always wrong!

Had I but seen his glorious eye
Once light the clouds that 'wilder me,
I ne'er had raised this coward cry
To cease to think and cease to be—

I ne'er had called oblivion blest,
Nor stretching eager hands to Death
Implored to change for senseless rest
This sentient soul, this living breath.

O let me die, that power and will
Their cruel strife may close,
And conquered good and conquered ill
Be lost in one repose.

It's over now; I've known it all;
I'll hide it in my heart no more,
But back again that night recall,
And think the fearful vision o'er.

The evening sun, in cloudless shine,
Has passed from summer's heaven divine;
And dark the shades of twilight grew,
And stars were in the depth of blue;

And in the heath on mountains far
From human eye and human care,
With thoughtful heart and tearful eye
I sadly watched that solemn sky.

I've been wandering in the greenwoods,
And mid flowery, smiling plains;
I've been listening to the dark floods,
To the thrush's trilling strains.

I have gathered the pale primrose,
And the purple violet sweet;
I've been where the asphodel grows,
And where lives the red deer fleet.

I've been to the distant mountain,
To the silver singing rill,
By the crystal murmuring fountain,
And the shady, verdant hill.

I've been where the poplar is springing
From the fair enamelled ground,
Where the nightingale is singing
With a solemn, plaintive sound

In the earth, the earth, thou shalt be laid,
A grey stone standing over thee;
Black mould beneath thee spread
And black mould to cover thee.

"Well, there is rest there,
So fast come thy prophecy;
The time when my sunny hair
Shall with grass roots twined be."

But cold, cold is that resting place,
Shut out from Joy and Liberty,
And all who loved thy living face
Will shrink from its gloom and thee.

"Not so: here the world is chill,
And sworn friends fall from me;
But there, they'll own me still
And prize my memory."

Farewell, then, all that love,
All that deep sympathy:
Sleep on; heaven laughs above,
Earth never misses thee.

Turf-sod and tombstone drear
Part human company;
One heart broke only there—
That heart was worthy thee!

Yes, holy be thy resting place
Wherever thou may'st lie;
The sweetest winds breathe on thy face,
The softest of the sky.

And will not guardian Angels send
Kind dreams and thoughts of love,
Though I no more may watchful bend
Thy longed repose above?

And will not heaven bestow
A beam of glory there
That summer's grass more green may grow,
And summer's flowers more fair?

Farewell, farewell, 'tis hard to part
Yet, loved one, it must be:
I would not rend another heart
Not even by blessing thee.

Go! we must break affection's chain,
Forget the hopes of years:
Nay, grieve not—willest thou remain
To waken wilder tears?

This wild breeze with thee and me
Roved in the dawning day;
And thou shouldest be where it shall be
Ere evening, far away

Shed no tears o'er that tomb
For there are Angels weeping;
Mourn not him whose doom
Heaven itself is mourning.

Look how in sable gloom
The clouds are earthward sweeping,
And earth receives them home,
Even darker clouds returning.

Is it when good men die
That sorrow wakes above?
Grieve saints when other spirits fly
To swell their choir of love?

Ah no, with louder sound
The golden harp strings quiver
When good men gain the happy ground
Where they must dwell for ever.

But he who slumbers there,
His bark will strive no more
Across the waters of despair
To reach that glorious shore.

The time of grace is past
And mercy scorned and tried
Forsakes to utter wrath at last
The soul so steeled by pride.

That wrath will never spare,
Will never pity know,
Will mock its victim's maddened prayer,
Will triumph in his woe.

Shut from his Maker's smile
The accursed man shall be:
For mercy reigns a little while,
But hate eternally.

I did not sleep; 'twas noon of day,
I saw the burning sunshine fall,
The long grass bending where I lay,
The blue sky brooding over all.

I heard the mellow hum of bees
And singing birds and sighing trees,
And far away in woody dell
The Music of the Sabbath bell.

I did not dream; remembrance still
Clasped round my heart its fetters chill;
But I am sure the soul is free
To leave its clay a little while,
Or how in exile misery
Could I have seen my country smile?

In English fields my limbs were laid
With English turf beneath my head;
My spirit wandered o'er that shore
Where nought but it may wander more.

Yet if the soul can thus return
I need not and I will not mourn;
And vainly did you drive me far
With leagues of ocean stretched between:
My mortal flesh you might debar,
But not the eternal fire within.

My Monarch died to rule forever
A heart that can forget him never;
And dear to me, aye, double dear,
Though shut within the silent tomb,
His name shall be for whom I bear
This long-sustained and hopeless doom.

And brighter in the hour of woe
Than in the blaze of victory's pride,
That glory shedding star shall glow
For which we fought and bled and died.

O thy bright eyes must answer now,
When Reason, with a scornful brow,
Is mocking at my overthrow;
O thy sweet tongue must plead for me
And tell why I have chosen thee!

Stern Reason is to judgement come
Arrayed in all her forms of gloom:
Wilt thou my advocate be dumb?
No, radiant angel, speak and say
Why I did cast the world away;

Why I have persevered to shun
The common paths that others run;
And on a strange road journeyed on
Heedless alike of Wealth and Power—
Of Glory's wreath and Pleasure's flower.

These once indeed seemed Beings divine,
And they perchance heard vows of mine
And saw my offerings on their shrine—
But, careless gifts are seldom prized,
And mine were worthily despised;

So with a ready heart I swore
To seek their altar-stone no more,
And gave my spirit to adore
Thee, ever present, phantom thing—
My slave, my comrade, and my King!

A slave because I rule thee still;
Incline thee to my changeful will
And make thy influence good or ill—
A comrade, for by day and night
Thou art my intimate delight—

My Darling Pain that wounds and sears
And wrings a blessing out from tears
By deadening me to earthly cares;
And yet, a king—though prudence well
Have taught thy subject to rebel.

And am I wrong to worship where
Faith cannot doubt nor Hope despair
Since my own soul can grant my prayer?
Speak, God of Visions, plead for me
And tell why I have chosen thee!

And like myself lone, wholly lone,
It sees the day's long sunshine glow;
And like myself it makes its moan
In unexhausted woe.

Give we the hills our equal prayer:
Earth's breezy hills and heaven's blue sea;
We ask for nothing further here
But our own hearts and liberty.

Ah! could my hand unlock its chain,
How gladly would I watch it soar,
And ne'er regret and ne'er complain
To see its shining eyes no more.

But let me think that if today
It pines in cold captivity,
Tomorrow both shall soar away,
Eternally, entirely Free.

Will the day be bright or cloudy?
Sweetly has its dawn begun;
But the heaven may shake with thunder
Ere the setting of the sun.

Lady, watch Apollo's journey:
Thus thy firstborn's course shall be—
If his beams through summer vapours
Warm the earth all placidly,
Her days shall pass like a pleasant dream
In sweet tranquility.

If it darken, if a shadow
Quench his rays and summon rain,
Flowers may open, buds may blossom:
Bud and flower alike are vain;
Her days shall pass like a mournful story
In care and tears and pain.

If the wind be fresh and free,
The wide skies clear and cloudless blue,
The woods and fields and golden flowers
Sparkling in sunshine and in dew,
Her days shall pass in Glory's light
The world's drear desert through.

How clear she shines! How quietly
I lie beneath her guardian light
While Heaven and Earth are whispering me,
"To-morrow wake, but dream to-night."

Yes, Fancy, come, my Fairy love!
These throbbing temples, softly kiss;
And bend my lonely couch above
And bring me rest and bring me bliss.

The world is going — Dark world, adieu!
Grim world, conceal thee till the day;
The heart thou canst not all subdue
Must still resist if thou delay!

Thy love I will not, will not share;
Thy hatred only wakes a smile;
Thy griefs may wound—thy wrongs may tear,
But, oh, thy lies shall ne'er beguile!

While gazing on the stars that glow
Above me in that stormless sea,
I long to hope that all the woe
Creation knows, is held in thee!

And this shall be my dream to-night—
I'll think the heaven of glorious spheres
Is rolling on its course of light
In endless bliss through endless years;

I'll think there's not one world above,
Far as these straining eyes can see,
Where Wisdom ever laughed at Love,
Or Virtue crouched to Infamy;

Where, writhing 'neath the strokes of Fate,
The mangled wretch was forced to smile;
To match his patience 'gainst her hate,
His heart rebellious all the while;

Where Pleasure still will lead to wrong,
And helpless Reason warn in vain;
And Truth is weak and Treachery strong,
And Joy the surest path to Pain;

And Peace, the lethargy of grief;
And Hope, a phantom of the soul;
And Life, a labour void and brief;
And Death, the despot of the whole!

Aye, there it is! It wakes to-night
Sweet thoughts that will not die
And feeling's fires flash all as bright
As in the years gone by!

And I can tell by thine altered cheek
And by thy kindled gaze
And by the words thou scarce dost speak,
How wildly fancy plays.

Yes, I could swear that glorious wind
Has swept the world aside,
Has dashed its memory from thy mind
Like foam-bells from the tide—

And thou art now a spirit pouring
Thy presence into all—
The essence of the Tempest's roaring
And of the Tempest's fall—

A universal influence
From Thine own influence free;
A principle of life, intense,
Lost to mortality.

Thus truly when that breast is cold
Thy prisoned soul shall rise,
The dungeon mingle with the mould—
The captive with the skies.

I see around me tombstones grey
Stretching their shadows far away.
Beneath the turf my footsteps tread
Lie low and lone the silent dead;
Beneath the turf, beneath the mould—
Forever dark, forever cold,
And my eyes cannot hold the tears
That memory hoards from vanished years;
For Time and Death and Mortal pain
Give wounds that will not heal again.
Let me remember half the woe
I've seen and heard and felt below,
And Heaven itself, so pure and blest,
Could never give my spirit rest.
Sweet land of light! thy children fair
Know nought akin to our despair;
Nor have they felt, nor can they tell
What tenants haunt each mortal cell,
What gloomy guests we hold within—
Torments and madness, tears and sin!
Well, may they live in ecstasy
Their long eternity of joy;
At least we would not bring them down
With us to weep, with us to groan.

No—Earth would wish no other sphere
To taste her cup of sufferings drear;
She turns from Heaven a careless eye
And only mourns that we must die!
Ah mother, what shall comfort thee
In all this boundless misery?
To cheer our eager eyes a while
We see thee smile; how fondly smile!
But who reads not through that tender glow
Thy deep, unutterable woe?
Indeed, no dazzling land above
Can cheat thee of thy children's love.
We all, in life's departing shine,
Our last dear longings blend with thine;
And struggle still and strive to trace
With clouded gaze, they darling's face.
We would not leave our native home
For any world beyond the Tomb.
No—rather on thy kindly breast
Let us be laid in lasting rest;
Or waken but to share with thee
A mutual immortality.

O between distress and pleasure
Fond affection cannot be;
Wretched hearts in vain would treasure
Friendship's joys when others flee.

Well I know thine eye would never
Smile, while mine grieved, willingly;
Yet I know thine eye for ever
Could not weep in sympathy.

Let us part, the time is over
When I thought and felt like thee;
I will be an Ocean rover,
I will sail the desert sea.

Isles there are beyond its billow;
Lands where woe may wander free;
And, beloved, thy midnight pillow
Will be soft unwatched by me.

Not on earth returning morrow
When thy heart bounds ardently
Need'st thou then dissemble sorrow,
Marking my despondency.

Day by day some dreary token
Will forsake thy memory
Till at last, all old links broken,
I shall be a dream to thee.

Alone I sat; the summer day
Had died in smiling light away;
I saw it die. I watched it fade
From misty hill and breezeless glade;

And thoughts in my soul were gushing.
And my heart bowed beneath their power;
And tears within my eyes were rushing
Because I could not speak the feeling,
The solemn joy around me stealing
In that divine, untroubled hour.

I asked myself, "O why has heaven
Denied the precious gift to me,
The glorious gift to many given
To speak their thoughts in poetry?

"Dreams have encircled me," I said,
"From careless childhood's sunny time;
Visions by ardent fancy fed
Since life was in its morning prime."

But now, when I had hoped to sing,
My fingers strike a tuneless string;
And still the burden of the strain
Is "Strive no more; 'tis all in vain."

How long will you remain? The midnight hour
Has tolled the last note from the minster tower.
Come, come: the fire is dead, the lamp burns low,
Your eyelids droop, a weight is on your brow.
Your cold hands hardly hold the useless pen;
Come: morn will give recovered strength again.

"No: let me linger; leave me, let me be
A little long in this reverie.
I'm happy now, and would you tear away
My blissful dream, that never comes with day;
A vision dear, though false, for well my mind
Knows what a bitter waking waits behind?"

"Can there be pleasure in this shadowy room
With windows yawning on intenser gloom,
And such a dreary wind so bleakly sweeping
Round walls where only you are vigil keeping?
Besides, your face hast not a sign of joy,
And more than tearful sorrow fills your eye.
Look on those woods, look on that heaven lorn,
And think how changed they'll be to-morrow morn:
The dome of heaven expanding bright and blue,
The leaves, the green grass, sprinkled thick with dew,
And wet mists rising on the river's breast,
And wild birds bursting from their songless nest,
And your own children's merry voices chasing
The fancies grief, not pleasure, has been tracing."

"Aye, speak of these, but can you tell me why
Day breathes such beauty over earth and sky,
And waking sounds revive, restore again
The hearts that all night long have throbbed in pain?
Is it not that the sunshine and the wind
Lure from its self the mourner's woe-worn mind;
And all the joyous music breathing by,
And all the splendour of that cloudless sky,
Re-give him shadowy gleams of infancy,
And draw his tired gaze from futurity?

I'll come when thou are saddest,
Laid alone in the darkened room;
When the mad day's mirth has vanished,
And the smile of joy is banished
From evening's chilly gloom.

I'll come when the heart's real feeling
Has entire, unbiased sway,
And my influence o'er thee stealing,
Grief deepening, joy congealing,
Shall bear thy soul away.

Listen, 'tis just the hour,
The awful time for thee;
Dost thou not feel upon thy soul
A flood of strange sensations roll,
Forerunners of a sterner power,
Heralds of me?

And now the house-dog stretched once more
His limbs upon the glowing floor;
The children half resumed their play
Though from the warm hearth scared away.
The goodwife left her spinning-wheel,
And spread with smiles the evening meal;
The shepherd placed a seat and pressed
To their poor fare his unknown guest.
And he unclasped his mantle now,
And raised the covering from his brow;
Said, "Voyagers by land and sea
Were seldom feasted daintily";
And rebuked his host by adding stern
He'd no refinement to unlearn.
A silence settled on the room;
The cheerful welcome sank to gloom;
But not those words, though cold and high,
So froze their hospitable joy.
No—there was something in his face,
Some nameless thing they could not trace,
And something in his voice's tone
Which turned their blood as chill as stone.
The ringlets of his long black hair
Fell o'er a cheek most ghastly fair.
Youthful he seemed—but worn as they
Who spend too soon their youthful day.
When his glance drooped, 'twas hard to quell
Unbidden feelings' sudden swell;
And pity scarce her tears could hide,
So sweet that brow, with all its pride;
But when upraised his eye would dart
An icy shudder through the heart.

Compassion changed to horror then
And fear to meet that gaze again.
It was not hatred's tiger-glare,
Nor the wild anguish of despair;
It was not useless misery
Which mocks at friendship's sympathy.
No—lightning all unearthly shone
Deep in that dark eye's circling zone,
Such withering lightning as we deem
None but a spectre's look may beam;
And glad they were when he turned away
And wrapped him in his mantle grey,
Leant down his head upon his arm
And veiled from view his basilisk charm.

May flowers are opening
And leaves unfolding free;
There are bees in every blossom
And birds on every tree.

The sun is gladly shining,
The stream sings merrily,
And I only am pining—
And all is dark to me.

O cold, cold is my heart!
It will not, cannot rise;
It feels no sympathy
With those refulgent skies.

Dead, dead is my joy,
I long to be at rest;
I wish the damp earth covered
This desolate breast.

If I were quite alone,
It might not be so drear,
When all hope was gone;
At least I could not fear.

But the glad eyes around me
Must weep as mine have done,
And I must see the same gloom
Eclipse their morning sun.

If heaven would rain on me
That future storm of care,
So their fond hearts were free
I'd be content to bear.

Alas! as lightning withers
The young and aged tree,
Both they and I shall fall beneath
The fate we cannot flee.

The blue bell is the sweetest flower
That waves in summer air;
Its blossoms have the mightiest power
To soothe my spirit's care.

There is a spell in purple heath
Too wildly, sadly dear;
The violet has a fragrant breath
But fragrance will not cheer.

The trees are bare, the sun is cold,
And seldom, seldom seen;
The heavens have lost their zone of gold
The earth its robe of green;

And ice upon the glancing stream
Has cast its sombre shade
And distant hills and valleys seem
In frozen mist arrayed.

The blue bell cannot charm me now,
The heath has lost its bloom
The violets in the glen below
They yield no sweet perfume.

But though I mourn the heather-bell
'Tis better far, away;
I know how fast my tears would swell
To see it smile to-day;

And that wood flower that hides so shy
Beneath its mossy stone
Its balmy scent and dewy eye:
'Tis not for them I moan.

It is the slight and stately stem,
The blossoms silvery blue,
The buds hid like a sapphire gem
In sheaths of emerald hue.

"Tis these that breathe upon my heart
A calm and softening spell
That if it makes the teardrop start
Has power to soothe as well.

For these I weep, so long divided
Through winter's dreary day,
In longing weep—but most when guided
On withered banks to stray.

If chilly then the light should fall
Adown the dreary sky
And gild the dank and darkened wall
With transient brilliancy,

How do I yearn, how do I pine
For the time of flowers to come,
And turn me from that fading shine
To mourn the fields of home.

Sleep brings no joy to me,
Remembrance never dies;
My soul is given to misery
And lives in sighs.

Sleep brings no rest to me;
The shadows of the dead
My waking eyes may never see
Surround my bed.

Sleep brings no hope to me;
In soundest sleep they come,
And with their doleful imagery
Deepen the gloom.

Sleep brings no strength to me,
No power renewed to brave—
I only sail a wilder sea—
A darker wave.

Sleep brings no friend to me
To soothe and aid to bear;
They all gaze, oh, how scornfully,
And I despair.

Sleep brings no wish to knit
My harassed heart beneath;
My only wish is to forget
In the sleep of death.

How still, how happy! Those are words
That once would scarce agree together;
I loved the plashing of the surge,
The changing heaven, the breezy weather,

More than smooth seas and cloudless skies
And solemn, soothing, softened airs
That in the forest woke no sighs
And from the green spray shook no tears.

How still, how happy! Now I feel
Where silence dwells is sweeter far
Than laughing mirth's most joyous swell
However pure its raptures are.

Come, sit down on this sunny stone:
'Tis wintry light o'er flowerless moors—
But sit—for we are all alone
And clear expand heaven's breathless shores.

I could think in the withered grass
Spring's budding wreaths we might discern;
The violet's eye might shyly flash
And young leaves shoot among the fern.

It is but thought—full many a night
The snow shall clothe those hills afar
And storms shall add a drearier blight
And winds shall wage a wilder war,

Before the lark may herald in
Fresh foliage twined with blossoms fair
And summer days again begin
Their glory-haloed crown to wear.

Yet my heart loves December's smile
As much as July's golden beam;
Then let us sit and watch while
Blue ice curdles on the stream.

No coward soul is mine
No trembler in the world's storm-troubled sphere;
I see Heaven's glories shine
And Faith shines equal arming me from Fear.

O God within my breast,
Almighty ever-present Deity;
Life, that in me hast rest
As I—Undying Life—have power in Thee.

Vain are the thousand creeds
That move men's hearts—unutterably vain,
Worthless as withered weeds
Or idlest froth amid the boundless main—

To waken doubt in one
Holding so fast by thy infinity
So surely anchored on
The steadfast rock of Immortality.

With wide-embracing love
Thy spirit animates eternal years;
Pervades and broods above,
Changes, sustains, dissolves, creates and rears;

Though Earth and moon were gone
And suns and universes ceased to be,
And thou wert left alone
Every Existence would exist in thee.

There is not room for Death
Nor atom that his might could render void
Since thou are Being and Breath
And what thou art may never be destroyed.

Pencil Drawing by Emily Brontë
(Courtesy of Brontë Parsonage Museum, Haworth)

GONDAL

The Gondal poems constitute the bulk of the surviving works and should be read for what they are: brilliantly descriptive lyrical poems. For illustrative power they rival any epic, and knowing they are exclusively the product of imagination makes them all the more remarkable.

The poems were a joint effort between Emily and her sister, Anne. Began as a play when the girls were in their early-teens, it centered on the inhabitants of a mythical island in the North Pacific, their civil wars, their political rivalries, and their subsequent colonization and partitioning of Gaaldine, a South Pacific island. Because the play and the prose have been lost, as no doubt some of the poems, the story line is confusing. Characters appear and disappear, and incidents drop randomly into the plot. These poems, and some are obviously incomplete, were written over a long period (circa 1836-48). Emily apparently gave little thought to consistency, and the poems' raw and almost adolescent emotion suggests that they were therapeutic mental exercises to wile away the time, and not intended for publication. Although several were included in the *Bell* collection, the Gondal references were deleted.

Still few poets have captured the ravages of war and conquest, intrigue and tragedy as well. Emily Brontë never saw a battle, nor conspired against the throne, nor plotted assassination, nor marched in armies: she was never in love. But, she vividly describes all the aforesaid, and is especially adept at capturing the sorrow of conflict on the battlefield and in the heart. More than one of these poems would be appropriate as an Old Warrior eulogy, just as others are unrivaled laments of betrayal, lost causes, and shattered lives.

(NOTE: That Emily Brontë separated Gondal poems from her other works is clear: she kept them in a specifically marked diary. The debate over which poem was Gondal-inspired and which wasn't is entertaining but superfluous. All writers cannibalize, and Brontë is no different.)

The night was dark, yet winter breathed
With softened sighs on Gondal's shore;
And, though its wind repining grieved,
It chained the snow-swollen streams no more.

How deep into the wilderness
My horse had strayed, I cannot say;
But neither morsel nor caress
Would urge him farther on the way;

So, loosening from his neck the rein,
I set my worn companion free;
And billowy hill and boundless plain
Full soon divided him from me.

The sullen clouds lay all unbroken
And blackening round the horizon drear;
But still they gave no certain token
Of heavy rain or tempests near.

I paused, confounded and distressed;
Down in the heath my limbs I threw;
Yet wilder as I longed for rest
More wakeful heart and eyelids grew.

It was about the middle night,
And under such a starless dome,
When, gliding from the mountain's height,
I saw a shadowy spirit come.

Her wavy hair, on her shoulders bare,
It shone like soft clouds round the moon;
Her noiseless feet, like melting sleet,
Gleamed white a moment, then were gone.

"What seek you now, on this bleak moor's brow?
Where wanders that form from heaven descending?"
It was thus I said as, her graceful head,
The spirit above my couch was bending.

"This is my home, where whirlwinds blow,
Where snowdrifts round my path are swelling;
'Tis many a year, 'tis long ago,
Since I beheld another dwelling.

"When thick and fast the smothering blast
O'erwhelmed the hunter on the plain,
If my cheek grew pale in its loudest gale
May I never tread the hills again.

"The shepherd had died on the mountain side,
But my ready aid was near him then:
I led him back o'er the hidden track,
And gave him to his native glen.

"When tempests roar on the lonely shore,
I light my beacon with sea-weeds dry,
And it flings its fire through the darkness dire
And gladdens the sailor's hopeless eye.

"And the scattered sheep, I love to keep
Their timid forms to guard from harm;
I have a spell, and they know it well,
And I save them with a powerful charm.

"Thy own good steed on his friendless bed
A few hours since you left to die;
But I knelt by his side and the saddle untied,
And life returned to his glazing eye.

"And deem thou not that quite forgot
My mercy will forsake me now:
I bring thee care and not despair;
Abasement but not overthrow.

"To a silent home thy foot may come
And years may follow of toilsome pain;
But yet I swear by that burning tear
The loved shall meet on its hearth again."

Come hither, child—who gifted thee
With power to touch that string so well?
How darest thou rouse up thoughts in me,
Thoughts that I would, but cannot quell?

Nay, chide not, lady; long ago
I heard those notes in Ula's hall;
And, had I known they'd waken woe,
I'd weep, their music to recall.

But thus it was: one festal night,
When I was hardly six years old,
I stole away from crowds and light
And sought a chamber dark and cold.

I had no one to love me there;
I knew no comrade and no friend;
And so I went to sorrow where
Heaven, only heaven, saw me bend.

Loud blew the wind; 'twas sad to stay
From all that splendour barred away.
I imagined in the lonely room
A thousand forms of fearful gloom;

And, with my wet eyes raised on high,
I prayed to God that I might die.
Suddenly, in that silence drear,
A sound of music reached my ear;

And then a note; I hear it yet,
So full of soul, so deeply sweet,
I thought that Gabriel's self had come
To take me to my father's home.

Three times it rose, that seraph-strain,
Then died, nor lived ever again;
But still the words and still the tone
Swell round my heart when all alone.

A thousand sounds of happiness,
And only one of real distress,
One hardly uttered groan—
But that has hushed all vocal joy,
Eclipsed the glory of the sky,
And made me think that misery
Rules in our world alone!

About his face the sunshine glows,
And in his hair the south wind blows,
And violet and wild wood-rose
Are sweetly breathing near;
Nothing without suggests dismay,
If he could force his mind away
From tracking farther, day by day,
The desert of Despair.

Too truly agonized to weep,
His eyes are motionless as sleep;
His frequent sighs, long-drawn and deep,
Are anguish to my ear;
And I would soothe—but can I call
The cold corpse from its funeral pall,
And cause a gleam of hope to fall
With my consoling tear?

O Death, so many spirits driven
Through this false world, their all had given
To win the everlasting haven
To sufferers so divine—
Why didst thou smite the loved, the blest,
The ardent and the happy breast,
That, full of hope, desired not rest,
And shrank appalled from thine?

At least, since thou wilt not restore,
In mercy, launch one arrow more;
Life's conscious Death it wearies sore,
It tortures worse than thee.

Enough of storms have bowed his head:
Grant him at last a quiet bed,
Beside his early stricken dead—
Even where he yearns to be!

"Thou standest in the greenwood now
The place, the hour the same—
And here the fresh leaves gleam and glow
And there, down in the lake below,
The tiny ripples flame.

"The breeze sings like a summer breeze
Should sing in summer skies
And tower-like rocks and tent-like trees
In mingled glory rise.

"But where is he to-day, to-day?"
"O question not with me."
"I will not, Lady; only say
Where may thy lover be?

"Is he upon some distant shore
Or is he on the sea,
Or is the heart thou dost adore
A faithless heart to thee?

"The heart I love, whate'er betide,
Is faithful as the grave
And neither foreign lands divide
Nor yet the rolling wave."

"Then why should sorrow cloud that brow
And tears those eyes bedim?
Reply this once — is it that thou
Hast faithless been to him?"

"I gazed upon the cloudless moon
And loved her all the night
Till morning came and ardent noon,
Then I forgot her light—

No—not forgot—eternally
Remains its memory dear;
But could the day seem dark to me
Because the night was fair?

"I well may mourn that only one
Can light my future sky
Even though by such a radiant sun
My moon of life must die."

How few, of all the hearts that loved,
Are grieving for thee now!
And why should mine, tonight, be moved
With such a sense of woe?

Too often, thus, when left alone
Where none my thoughts can see,
Comes back a word, a passing tone
From thy strange history.

Sometimes I seem to see thee rise,
A glorious child again—
All virtues beaming from thine eyes
That ever honoured men—

Courage and Truth, a generous breast
Where Love and Gladness lay;
A being whose very Memory blest
And made the mourner gay.

O, fairly spread thy early sail,
And fresh and pure and free
Was the first impulse of the gale
That urged life's wave for thee!

Why did the pilot, too confiding,
Dream o'er that Ocean's foam,
And trust in Pleasure's careless guiding
To bring his vessel home?

For well he knew what dangers frowned,
What mists would gather dim;
What rocks and shelves and sands lay round
Between his port and him.

The very brightness of the sun,
The splendour of the main,
The wind that bore him wildly on
Should not have warned in vain.

An anxious gazer from the shore,
I marked the whitening wave,
And wept above thy fate the more
Because I could not save.

It wrecks not now, when all is over;
But yet my heart will be
A mourner still, though friend and lover
Have both forgotten thee!

The linnet in the rocky dells,
The moor-lark in the air,
The bee among the heather-bells
That hide my lady fair:

The wild deer browse above her breast;
The wild birds raise their brood;
And they, her smiles of love caressed,
Have left her solitude!

I ween, that when the grave's dark wall
Did first her form retain,
They thought their hearts could ne'er recall
The light of joy again.

They thought the tide of grief would flow
Unchecked through future years,
But where is all their anguish now,
And where are all their tears?

Well, let them fight for Honour's breath,
Or Pleasure's shade pursue—
The Dweller in the land of Death
Is changed and careless too.

And if their eyes should watch and weep
Till sorrow's source were dry,
She would not, in her tranquil sleep,
Return a single sigh.

Blow, west wind, by the lonely mound,
And murmur, summer streams,
There is no need of other sound
To soothe my Lady's dreams.

I've seen this dell in July's shine
As lovely as an angel's dream;
Above, heaven's depth of blue divine;
Around, the evening's golden beam.

I've seen the purple heather-bell
Look out by many a storm-worn stone;
And oh, I've seen such music swell,
Such wild notes wake these passes lone—

So soft, yet so intensely felt,
So low, yet so distinctly heard,
My breath would pause, my eyes would melt,
And my tears dew the green heath sward.

I'd linger here a summer day,
Not care how fast the hours flew by,
Nor mark the sun's departing ray
Smile sadly glorious from the sky.

Then, then I might have laid thee down
And deemed thy sleep would gentle be;
I might have left thee, darling one,
And thought thy God was guarding thee!

But now there is no wandering glow,
No gleam to say that God is nigh;
And coldly spreads thy couch of snow,
And harshly sounds thy lullaby.

Forests of heather, dark and long,
Wave their brown, branching arms above,
And they must soothe thee with their song,
And they must shield my child of love!

Alas, the flakes are heavily falling;
They cover fast each guardian crest;
And chilly white their shroud is palling
Thy frozen limbs and freezing breast.

Wakes up the storm more madly wild,
The mountain drifts are tossed on high—
Farewell, unblessed, unfriended child,
I cannot bear to watch thee die.

It is not pride, it is not shame,
That makes her leave the gorgeous hall;
And though neglect her heart might tame
She mourns not for her sudden fall.

'Tis true she stands among the crowd
An unmarked and an unloved child,
While each young comrade, blithe and proud,
Glides through the maze of pleasure wild.

And all do homage to their will,
And all seem glad their voice to hear;
She heeds not that, but hardly still
Her eye can hold the quivering tear.

What made her weep, what made her glide
Out to park this dreary day,
And cast her jewelled chains aside,
And seek a rough and lonely way,

And down beneath a cedar's shade
On the wet grass regardless lie,
With nothing but its gloomy head
Between her and the showery sky?

I saw her stand in the gallery long,
Watching the little children there,
As they were playing the pillars among
And bounding down the marble stair.

Come, the wind may never again
Blow as now it blows for us;
And the stars may never again shine as now they shine;
Long before October returns,
Seas of blood will have parted us;
And you must crush the love in your heart,
And I the love in mine!

For face to face will our kindred stand,
And as they are so shall we be;
Forgetting how the same sweet earth has borne and nourished all—
One must fight for the people's power,
And one for the rights of Royalty;
And each be ready to give his life
To work the other's fall.

The chance of war we cannot shun,
Nor would we shrink from our fathers' cause,
Nor dread Death more because the hand that gives it may be dear;
We must bear to see Ambition rule
Over Love, with his iron laws;
Must yield our blood for a stranger's sake, and refuse ourselves a tear!

So, the wind may never again
Blow as now it blows for us,
And the stars may never again shine as now they shine;
Next October, the cannon's roar
From hostile ranks may be urging us—
Me to strike for your life's blood, and you to strike for mine.

Thy sun is near meridian height,
And my sun sinks in endless night;
But, if that night bring only sleep,
Then I shall rest, while thou wilt weep.

And say not that my early tomb
Will give me to a darker doom:
Shall these long, agonizing years
Be punished by eternal tears?

No; that I feel can never be;
A God of hate could hardly bear
To watch through all eternity
His own creations dread despair!

The pangs that wring my mortal breast,
Must claim from Justice lasting rest;
Enough, that this departing breath
Will pass in anguish worse than death.

If I have sinned, long, long ago
That sin was purified by woe:
I've suffered on through night and day;
I've trod a dark and frightful way.

Earth's wilderness was round me spread;
Heaven's tempests beat my naked head;
I did not kneel: in vain would prayer
Have sought one gleam of mercy there!

How could I ask for pitying love,
When that grim concave frowned above,
Hoarding its lightnings to destroy
My only and my priceless joy?

They struck—and long may Eden shine
Ere I would call its glories mine:
All Heaven's undreamt felicity
Could never blot the past from me.

No: years may cloud and death may sever,
But what is done is done forever;
And thou, false friend and treacherous guide,
Go, sate thy cruel heart with pride.

Go, load my memory with shame;
Speak but to curse my hated name;
My tortured limbs in dungeons bind,
And spare my life to kill my mind.

Leave me in chains and darkness now;
And when my very soul is worn,
When reason's light has left my brow,
And madness cannot feel thy scorn,

Then come again—thou wilt not shrink;
I know thy soul is free from fear—
The last full cup of triumph drink,
Before the blank of death be there.

Thy raving, dying victim see,
Lost, cursed, degraded, all for thee!
Gaze on the wretch, recall to mind
His golden days left long behind.

Does memory sleep in Lethean rest?
Or wakes its whisper in thy breast?
O memory, wake! Let scenes return
That even her haughty heart must mourn!

Reveal, where o'er a lone green wood
The moon of summer pours,
Far down from heaven, its silver flood,
On deep Elderno's shores.

There, lingering in the wild embrace
Youth's warm affections gave,
She sits and fondly seems to trace
His features in the wave.

And while on that reflected face
Her eyes intently dwell,
"Fernando, sing tonight," she says,
"The lays I love so well."

He smiles and sings, though every air
Betrays the faith of yesterday;
His soul is glad to cast for her
Virtue and faith and Heaven away.

Well thou hast paid me back my love!
But there be a God above
Whose arm is strong, whose word is true,
This hell shall wring thy spirit too!

Silent is the House—all are laid asleep;
One, alone, looks out o'er the snow wreaths deep;
Watching every cloud, dreading every breeze
That whirls the 'wildering drifts and bends the groaning trees.

Cheerful is the hearth, soft the matted floor;
Not one shivering gust creeps through pane or door;
The little lamp burns straight, its rays shoot strong and far;
I trim it well to be the Wanderer's guiding star.

Frown, my haughty sire; chide, my angry dame;
Set your slaves to spy, threaten me with shame:
But neither sire nor dame, nor prying serf shall know
What angel nightly tracks that waste of winter snow.

In the dungeon crypts idly did I stray,
Reckless of the lives wasting there away;
"Draw the ponderous bars; open, Warder stern!"
He dare not say me nay—the hinges harshly turn.

"Our guests are darkly lodged," I whispered, gazing through
The vault whose grated eye showed heaven more grey than blue.
(This was when glad spring laughed in awaking pride.)
"Aye, darkly lodged enough!" returned my sullen guide.

Then, God forgive my youth, forgive my careless tongue!
I scoffed, as the chill chains on the damp flagstones rung;
"Confined in triple walls, art thou so much to fear,
That we must bind thee down and clench thy fetters here?"

The captive raised her face; it was as soft and mild
As sculptured marble saint or slumbering, unweaned child;
It was so soft and mild, it was so sweet and fair,
Pain could not trace a line nor grief a shadow there!

The captive raised her hand and pressed it to her brow:
"I have been struck," she said, "and I am suffering now;
Yet these are little worth, your bolts and irons strong;
And were they forged in steel they could not hold me long."

Hoarse laughed the jailor grim: "Shall I be won to hear;
Dost think, fond dreaming wretch, that I shall grant thy prayer?
Or, better still, wilt melt my master's heart with groans?
Ah, sooner might the sun thaw down these granite stones!

"My master's voice is low, his aspect bland and kind,
But hard as hardest flint the soul that lurks behind;
And I am rough and rude, yet not more rough to see
Than is the hidden ghost that has its home in me!"

About her lips there played a smile of almost scorn:
"My friend," she gently said, "you have not heard me mourn;
When you my kindred's lives, my lost life, can restore,
Then may I weep and sue—but never, Friend, before!"

Her head sank on her hands; its fair curls swept the ground;
The dungeon seemed to swim in strange confusion round—
"Is she so near to death?" I murmured, half aloud,
And, kneeling, parted back the floating golden cloud.

Alas, how former days upon my heart were borne;
How memory mirrored then the prisoner's joyous morn:
Too blithe, too loving child, too warmly, wildly gay!
Was that the wintry close of thy celestial May?

She knew me and she sighed, "Lord Julian, can it be,
Of all my playmates, you alone remember me?
Nay, start not at my words, unless you deem it shame
To own, from conquered foe, a once familiar name.

"I cannot wonder now at ought the world will do,
And insult and contempt I lightly brook from you,
Since those, who vowed away their souls to win my love,
Around this living grave like utter strangers move!

"Nor has one voice been raised to plead that I might die,
Not buried under earth but in the open sky;
By ball or speedy knife or headsman's skilful blow—
A quick and welcome pang instead of lingering woe!

"Still, let my tyrants know, I am not doomed to wear
Year after year in gloom and desolate despair;
A messenger of Hope comes every night to me,
And offers, for short life, eternal liberty.

He comes with western winds, with evening's wandering airs,
With that clear dusk of heaven that brings the thickest stars;
Winds take a pensive tone, and stars a tender fire,
And visions rise and change that kill me with desire—

"Desire for nothing known in my maturer years
When joy grew mad with awe at counting future tears;
When, if my spirit's sky was full of flashes warm,
I knew not whence they came, from sun or thunderstorm;

"But first a hush of peace, a soundless calm descends;
The struggle of distress and fierce impatience ends;
Mute music soothes my breast—unuttered harmony
That I could never dream till earth was lost to me.

"Then dawns the Invisible, the Unseen its truth reveals;
My outward sense is gone, my inward essence feels—
Its wings are almost free, its home, its harbour found;
Measuring the gulf it stoops and dares the final bound!

"Oh, dreadful is the check—intense the agony
When the ear begins to hear and the eye begins to see;
When the pulse begins to throb, the brain to think again,
The soul to feel the flesh and the flesh to feel the chain!

"Yet I would lose no sting, would wish no torture less;
The more that anguish racks the earlier it will bless;
And robed in fires of Hell, or bright with heavenly shine,
If it but herald Death, the vision is divine."

She ceased to speak, and I, unanswering, watched her there,
Not daring now to touch one lock of silken hair—
As I had knelt in scorn, on the dank floor I knelt still,
My fingers in the links of that iron hard and chill.

I heard, and yet heard not, the surly keeper growl;
I saw, yet did not see, the flagstone damp and foul.
The keeper, to and fro, paced by the bolted door
And shivered as he walked and, as he shivered, swore.

While my cheek glowed in flame, I marked that he did rave
Of air that froze his blood, and moisture like the grave—
"We have been two hours good!" he muttered peevishly;
Then, loosing off his belt the rusty dungeon key,

He said, "You may be pleased, Lord Julian, still to stay,
But duty will not let me linger here all day;
If I might go, I'd leave this badge of mine with you,
Not doubting that you'd prove a jailor stern and true."

I took the proffered charge; the captive's drooping lid
Beneath its shady lash a sudden lightning hid:
Earth's hope was not so dead, heaven's home was not so dear;
I read it in that flash of longing quelled by fear.

Then like a tender child whose hand did just enfold,
Safe in its eager grasp, a bird it wept to hold,
When pierced with one wild glance from the troubled hazel eye,
It gushes into tears and lets its treasure fly.

Thus ruth and selfish love together striving tore
The heart all newly taught to pity and adore;
If I should break the chain, I felt my bird would go;
Yet I must break the chain or seal the prisoner's woe.

Short strife, what rest could soothe—what peace could visit me
While she lay pining there for Death to set her free?
"Rochelle, the dungeons teem with foes to gorge our hate—
Thou art too young to die by such a bitter fate!"

With hurried blow on blow, I struck the fetters through,
Regardless how that deed my after hours might rue.
Oh, I was over-blest by the warm unasked embrace—
By the smile of grateful joy that lit her angel face!

And I was over-blest—aye, more than I could dream
When, faint, she turned aside from noon's unwonted beam;
When though the cage was wide—the heaven around it lay—
Its pinion would not waft my wounded dove away.

Through thirteen anxious weeks of terror-blent delight
I guarded her by day and guarded her by night,
While foes were prowling near and Death gazed greedily
And only Hope remained a faithful friend to me.

Then oft with taunting smile I heard my kindred tell—
How Julian loved his hearth and sheltering roof-tree well;
How the trumpet's voice might call, the battle standard wave,
But Julian had no heart to fill a patriot's grave.

And I, who am so quick to answer sneer with sneer;
So ready to condemn, to scorn, a coward's fear,
I held my peace like one whose conscience keeps him dumb,
And saw my kinsmen go—and lingered still at home.

Another hand than mine my rightful banner held
And gathered my renown on Freedom's crimson field;
Yet I had no desire the glorious prize to gain—
It needed braver nerve to face the world's disdain.

And by the patient strength that could that world defy,
By suffering, with calm mind, contempt and calumny;
By never-doubting love, unswerving constancy,
Rochelle, I earned at last an equal love from thee!

O Day! He cannot die
When thou so fair art shining;
O Sun! in such a glorious sky
So tranquilly declining,

"He cannot leave thee now
While fresh west winds are blowing,
And all around his youthful brow
Thy cheerful light is glowing!

"Edward, awake, awake!
The golden evening gleams
Warm and bright on Arden's lake,
Arouse thee from thy dreams!

"Besides thee, on my knee,
My dearest friend, I pray
That thou, to cross the eternal sea
Wouldst yet one hour delay!

"I hear its billows roar,
I see them foaming high,
But no glimpse of a further shore
Has blessed my straining eye.

"Believe not what they urge
Of Eden isles beyond;
Turn back, from that tempestuous surge,
To thy own native land!

"It is not Death, but pain
That struggles in thy breast;
Nay, rally, Edward, rouse again,
I cannot let thee rest!

One long look, that sore reproved me
For the woe I could not bear—
One mute look of suffering moved me
To repent my useless prayer;

And with sudden check, the heaving
Of distraction passed away;
Not a sign of further grieving
Stirred my soul that awful day.

Paled, at length, that sweet sun setting;
Sunk to peace the twilight breeze;
Summer dews fell softly, wetting
Glen and glade, and silent trees.

Then his eyes began to weary,
Weighed beneath a mortal sleep;
And their orbs grew strangely dreary,
Clouded, even as they would weep;

But they wept not, but they changed not,
Never moved and never closed;
Troubled still, and still they ranged not,
Wandered not, nor yet reposed!

So I knew that he was dying—
Stooped and raised his languid head—
Felt no breath and heard no sighing,
So, I knew that he was dead.

The moon is full this winter night;
The stars are clear though few;
And every window glistens bright
With leaves of frozen dew.

The sweet moon through your lattice gleams
And lights your room like day;
And there you pass in happy dreams
The peaceful hours away;

While I, with effort hardly quelling
The anguish in my breast,
Wander about the silent dwelling
And cannot think of rest.

The old clock in the gloomy hall
Ticks on from hour to hour,
And every time its measured call
Seems lingering slow and slower.

And O how slow that keen-eyed star
Has tracked the chilly grey!
What watching yet, how very far
The morning lies away!

Without your chamber door I stand:
Love, are you slumbering still?
My cold heart underneath my hand
Has almost ceased to thrill.

Bleak, bleak the east wind sobs and sighs
And drowns the turret bell
Whose sad note, undistinguished, dies
Unheard, like my farewell.

Tomorrow Scorn will blight my name
And Hate will trample me—
Will load me with a coward's shame:
A Traitor's perjury!

False Friends will launch their covert sneers;
True friends will wish me dead;
And I shall cause the bitterest tears
That you have ever shed.

The dark deeds of my outlawed race
Will then like virtues shine;
And men will pardon their disgrace,
Beside the guilt of mine;

For who forgives the accursed crime
Of dastard treachery?
Rebellion in its chosen time
May Freedom's champion be;

Revenge may stain a righteous sword,
It may be just to slay;
But, Traitor, Traitor—from that word
All true breasts shrink away!

O I would give my heart to death,
To keep my honour fair:
Yet, I'll not give my inward Faith
My Honour's name to spare—

Not even to keep your priceless love,
Dare I, Beloved, deceive;
This treason should the future prove:
Then, only then, believe!

I know the path I ought to go;
I follow fearlessly,
Enquiring not what deeper woe
Stern Duty stores for me.

So foes pursue, and cold allies
Mistrust me, every one:
Let me be false in others' eyes
If faithful in my own.

Companions, all day long we've stood,
The wild winds restless blowing;
All day we've watched the darkened flood
Around our vessel flowing.

Sunshine has never smiled since morn,
And clouds have gathered drear,
And heavier hearts would feel forlorn
And weaker minds would fear.

But look in each young shipmate's eyes
Lit by the evening flame,
And see how little stormy skies
Our joyous blood can tame.

No glance the same expression wears,
No lip the same soft smile;
Yet kindness warms and courage cheers:
Nerves every breast the while.

It is the hour of dreaming now,
The red fire brightly gleams;
And sweetest in a red fire's glow
The hour of dreaming seems.

I may not trace the thoughts of all,
But some I read as well
As I can hear the ocean's fall
And sullen surging swell.

Edmund's swift soul is gone before:
It threads a forest wide,
Whose towers are bending to the shore
And gazing on the tide.

And one is there; I know the voice,
The thrilling, stirring tone
That makes his bounding pulse rejoice,
Yet makes not his alone.

Mine own hand longs to clasp her hand,
Mine eye to greet her eye;
Win, white sails, win Zedora's strand
And Ula's Eden sky.

Mary and Flora, oft their gaze
Is clouded pensively,
And what that earnest aspect says
Is all revealed to me.

"Tis but two years, or little more,
Since first they dared that main;
And such a night may well restore
That first time back again.

The smothered sigh, the lingering late,
The long-for, dreaded hour,
The parting at the moss-grown gate,
The last look on the tower:

I know they think of these, and then
The evening's gathering gloom,
And they alone, with foreign men
To guard their cabin room.

Alcona, in its changing mood
My soul will sometimes overfly
The long, long years of solitude
That 'twixt our time of meeting lie.

Hope and despair in turns arise
This doubting, dreading heart to move;
And now, 'mid smiles and bitter sighs,
Tell how I fear, tell how I love.

And now I say, "In Areon Hall—"
(Alas that such a dream should come,
When well I know, whate'er befall,
That Areon is no more my home.)

Yet, let me say, "In Areon Hall
The first fain red of morning shines,
And one right gladly to its call
The restless breath of grief resigns.

Her faded eye, her pallid face,
Would woo the soft, awaking wind;
All earth is breathing of the peace
She long has sought but cannot find.

How sweet it is to watch the mist
From that bright silent lake ascend,
And high o'er wood and mountain crest
With heaven's grey clouds as greyly blend.

How sweet it is to mark those clouds
Break brightly in the rising day;
To see the sober veil that shrouds
This summer morning melt away.

O sweet to some, but not to her;
Unmarkedst once at Nature's shrine,
She now kneels down a worshipper,
A mad adorer, love, to thine.

The time is come when hope, that long
Revived and sank, at length is o'er;
When faith in him, however strong,
Dare prompt her to believe no more.

The tears which day by day o'erflowed
Their heart-deep source begin to freeze;
And, as she gazes on the road
That glances through those spreading trees,

No throbbing flutter checks her breath
To mark a horseman hastening by;
Her haggard brow is calm as death,
And cold like death her dreary eye."

Were they shepherds, who sat all day
On that brown mountain side?
But neither staff nor dog had they,
Nor wooly flock to guide.

They were clothed in savage attire;
Their locks were dark and long;
And at each belt a weapon dire,
Like bandit-knife, was hung.

One was a woman, tall and fair;
A princess she might be,
From her stately form, and her features rare,
And her look of majesty.

But, oh, she had a sullen frown,
A lip of cruel scorn,
As sweet tears never melted down
Her cheeks since she was born!

'Twas well she had no sceptre to wield,
No subject land to sway:
Fear might have made her vassals yield,
But love had been far away.

Yet, love was even at her feet
In his most burning mood:
That Love which will the Wicked greet
As kindly as the Good—

And he was noble too, who bowed
So humbly by her side,
Entreating, till his eyes o'erflowed,
Her spirit's icy pride.

"Angelica, from my very birth
I have been nursed in strife:
And lived upon this weary Earth
A wanderer all my life.

"The baited tiger could not be
So much athirst for gore:
For men and laws have tortured me
'Till I can bear no more.

"The guiltless blood upon my hands
Will shut me out from Heaven;
And here, and even in foreign lands,
I cannot find a haven.

"And in all space, and in all time,
And through Eternity,
To aid a Spirit lost in crime,
I have no hope but thee.

"Yet will I swear, No saint on high
A truer faith could prove;
No angel, from that holy sky,
Could give thee purer love.

"For thee, through never-ending years,
I'd suffer endless pain;
But—only give me back my tears;
Return my love again!"

Many a time, unheeded, thus
The reckless man would pray;
But something woke an answering flush
On his lady's brow today;
And her eye flashed flame, as she turned to speak,
In concord with her reddening cheek:

"I've know a hundred kinds of love:
All made the loved one rue;
And what is thine that it should prove,
Than other love, more true?

"Listen; I've known a burning heart
To which my own was given;
Nay, not in passion; do not start—
Our love was love from heaven;
At least, if heavenly love be born
In the pure light of childhood's morn—
Long ere the poison-tainted air
From this world's plague-fen rises there.

"That heart was like a tropic sun
That kindles all it shines upon;
And never Magian devotee
Gave worship half so warm as I:
And never radiant bow could be
So welcome in a stormy sky.
My soul dwelt with her day and night:
She was my all-sufficing light,
My childhood's mate, my girlhood's guide,
My only blessing, only pride.

"But cursed be the very earth
That gave that fiend her fatal birth!
With her own hand she bent the bow
That laid my best affections low,
Then mocked my grief and scorned my prayers
And drowned my bloom of youth in tears.
Warning, reproaches, both were vain—
What recked she of another's pain?
My dearer self she would not spare—
From Honour's voice she turned his ear:
First made her love his only stay,
Then snatched the treacherous prop away.

Douglas, he pleaded bitterly;
He pleaded as you plead to me
For lifelong chains or timeless tomb
Or any but an Exile's doom.
We both were scorned—both sternly driven
To shelter 'neath a foreign heaven;
And darkens o'er that dreary time
A wildering dream of frenzied crime.
I will not now those days recall;
The oath within that caverned hall
And its fulfillment, those you know—
We both together struck the blow.
But—you can never know the pain
That my lost heart did then sustain,
When severed wide by guiltless gore
I felt that one could love no more!
Back, maddening thought!—The grave is deep
Where my Amedeus lies asleep,
And I have long forgot to weep.

"Now hear me: in these regions wild
I saw today my enemy.
Unarmed, as helpless as a child
She slumbered on a sunny lea.
Two friends—no other guard had she,
And they were wandering on the braes
And chasing in regardless glee
The wild goat o'er his dangerous ways.
My hand was raised—my knife was bare;
With stealthy tread I stole along;
But a wild bird sprang from his hidden lair
And woke her with a sudden song.
Yet moved she not: she only raised
Her lids and on the bright sun gazed,

And uttered such a dreary sigh
I thought just then she should not die
Since living was such misery.
Now, Douglas, for our hunted band—
For future joy and former woe—
Assist me with thy heart and hand
To send to hell my mortal foe.
Her friends fell first, that she may drain
A deeper cup of bitterer pain.
Yonder they stand and watch the waves
Dash in among the echoing caves—
Their farewell sight of earth and sea!
Come, Douglas, rise and go with me."

The lark sang clearly overhead,
And sweetly hummed the bee;
And softly, round their dying bed,
The wind blew from the sear.

Fair Surry would have raised her eyes
To see that water shine;
To see once more in mountain skies
The summer sun decline:

But ever, on her fading cheek,
The languid lid would close,
As weary that such light should break
Its much-desired repose.

And she was waning fast away—
Even Memory's voice grew dim;
Her former life's eventful day
Had dwindled to a dream;

And hardly could her mind recall
One thought of joy or pain;
That cloud was gathering over all
Which never clears again.

In vain, in vain; you need not gaze
Upon those features now!
That sinking head you need not raise,
Nor kiss that pulseless brow.

Let out the grief that chokes your breath;
Lord Lesley, set it free:
The sternest eye, for such a death,
Might fill with sympathy.

The tresses o'er her bosom spread
Were by a faint breeze blown:
"Her heart is beating," Lesley said;
"She is not really gone!"

And still that form he fondly pressed;
And still of hope he dreamed;
Nor marked how from his own young breast
Life's crimson current streamed.

At last, the sunshine left the ground;
The laden bee flew home;
The deep down sea, with sadder sound,
Impelled its waves to foam;

And the corpse grew heavy on his arm,
The starry heaven grew dim,
The summer night, so mild and warm,
Felt wintery chill to him.

A troubled shadow o'er his eye
Came down, and rested there;
The moors and sky went swimming by,
Confused and strange and drear.

He faintly prayed, "Oh, Death, delay
Thy last fell dart to throw,
Till I can hear my Sovereign say,
'The traitors' heads are low.'

"God, guard her life, since not to me
That dearest boon was given;
God, bless her arm with victory
Or bless not me with heaven!"

Then came the cry of agony,
The pang of parting pain;
And he had overpassed the sea
That can pass again.

Douglas leaned above the well,
Heather banks around him rose;
Bright and warm the sunshine fell
On that spot of sweet repose,

With the blue heaven bending o'er,
And the soft wind singing by,
And the clear stream evermore
Mingling harmony.

On the shady side reclined,
He watched its waters play,
And sound and sight had well combined
To banish gloom away.

A voice spoke near: "She's come," it said,
"And, Douglas, thou shalt be
My love, although the very dear
Should rise to rival thee!

"Now, only let thine arm be true
And nerved, like mine, to kill;
And Gondal's royal race shall rue
This day on Elmor Hill!"

They wait not long; the rustling heath
Betrays their royal foe;
With hurried step and panting breath
And cheek almost as white as death,
Augusta sprang below—

Yet marked she not where Douglas lay;
She only saw the well—
The tiny fountain, churning spray
Within its mossy cell.

"Oh, I have wrongs to pay," she cried,
"Give life, give vigor now!"
And, stooping by the water's side,
She drank its crystal flow.

And brightly, with that draught, came back
The glory of her matchless eye,
As, glancing o'er the moorland track.
She shook her head impatiently.

Nor shape, nor shade—the mountain flocks
Quietly feed in grassy dells;
Nor sound, except the distant rocks
Echoing to their bells.

She turns—she meets the Murderer's gaze;
Her own is scorched with a sudden blaze—
The blood streams down her brow;
The blood streams through her coal-black hair—
She strikes it off with little care;
She scarcely feels it flow;
For she had marked and known him too
And his own heart's ensanguined dew
Must slake her vengeance now!

False friend! no tongue save thine can tell
The mortal strife that then befell;
But, ere night darkened down,
The stream in silence sang once more;
And, on its green bank, bathed in gore,
Augusta lay alone!

False Love! no earthly eye did see,
Yet Heaven's pure eye regarded thee,
Where thy own Douglas bled—
How thou didst turn in mockery
From his last hopeless agony,
And leave the hungry hawk to be
Sole watcher of the dead!

Was it a deadly swoon?
Or was her spirit really gone?
And the cold corpse, beneath the moon,
Laid like another mass of dust and stone?

The moon was full that night,
The sky was almost like the day:
You might have seen the pulse's play
Upon her forehead white;

You might have seen the dear, dear sign of life
In her uncovered eye,
And her cheek changing in the mortal strife
Betwixt the pain to live and agony to die.

But nothing mutable was there;
The face, all deadly fair,
Showed a fixed impress of keen suffering past,
And the raised lid did show
No wandering gleam below
But a stark anguish, self-destroyed at last.

Long he gazed and held his breath,
Kneeling on the blood-stained heath;
Long he gazed those lids beneath
Looking into Death!

Not a word from his followers fell:
They stood by, mute and pale;
That black treason uttered well
Its own heart-harrowing tale.

But earth was bathed in other gore:
There were crimson drops across the moor;
And Lord Eldred, glancing round,
Saw those tokens on the ground:

132

"Bring him back!" he hoarsely said;
"Wounded is the traitor fled;
Vengeance may hold but minutes brief,
And you have all your lives for grief."

He is left alone—he sees the stars
Their quiet course continuing,
And, far, away, down Elmor scars
He hears the stream its waters fling.

That lulling monotone did sing
Of broken rock and shaggy glen,
Of welcome for the moorcock's wing;
But, not of wail for men!

Nothing in heaven or earth to show
One sign of sympathizing woe—
And nothing but that agony,
In her now unconscious eye,
To weigh upon the labouring breast
And prove she did not pass at rest.

But he who watched, in thought had gone,
Retracing back her lifetime flown:
Like sudden ghosts, to memory came
Full many a face and many a name,
Full many a heart, that, in the tomb,
He almost deemed might have throbbed again,
Had they but known her dreary doom,
Had they but seen their idol there,
A wreck of desolate despair,

Left to the wild birds of the air
And mountain winds and rain.
For him—no tear his stern eye shed
As he looked down upon the dead.

"Wild morn," he thought, "and doubtful noon;
But yet it was glorious sun,
Though comet-like its course was run.
That sun should never have been given
To burn and dazzle in the heaven,
Or night has quenched it far too soon!
And thou art gone—with all thy pride;
Thou, so adored, so deified!
Cold as the earth, unweeting now
Of love, or joy, or mortal woe.
For what thou wert I would not grieve,
But much for what thou wert to be—
That life so stormy and so brief,
That death has wronged us more than thee.
Thy passionate youth was nearly past,
The opening sea seemed smooth at last;
Yet vainly flowed the calmer wave
Since fate had not decreed to save.
And vain too must the sorrow be
Of those who live to mourn for thee;
But Gondal's foes shall not complain
That thy dear blood was poured in vain!"

The busy day has hurried by,
And hearts greet kindred hearts once more;
And swift the evening hours should fly,
But—what turns every gleaming eye
So often to the door,

And then so quick away—and why
Does sudden silence chill the room,
And laughter sink into a sigh,
And merry words to whispers die,
And gladness change to gloom?

O we are listening for a sound
We know shall ne'er be heard again;
Sweet voices in the halls resound,
Fair forms, fond faces gather round,
But all in vain—in vain!

Their feet shall never waken more
The echoes in these galleries wide,
Nor date the snow on the mountain's brow,
Nor skim the river's frozen flow,
Nor wander down its side.

They who have been our life—our soul—
Through summer-youth, from childhood's spring—
Who bound us in one vigorous whole
To stand 'gainst Tyranny's control
For ever triumphing—

Who bore the burnt of battle's fray:
The first to fight, the last to fall;
Whose mighty minds, with kindred ray,
Still led the van in Glory's way;
The idol chiefs of all—

They, they are gone! Not for a while
As golden suns at night decline
And even in death our grief beguile
Foretelling, with a rose-red smile,
How bright the morn will shine.

No; these dark towers are lone and lorn;
This very crowd is vacancy;
And we must watch and wait and mourn
And half look out for their return,
And think their forms we see;

And fancy music in our ear,
Such as their lips could only pour;
And think we feel their presence near,
And start to find they are not here,
And never shall be more!

King Julius left the south country
His banners all bravely flying;
His followers went out with Jubilee
But they shall return with sighing.

Loud arose the triumphal hymn
The drums were loudly rolling,
Yet you might have heard in distance dim
How a passing bell was tolling.

The sword so bright from battles won
With unseen rust is fretting,
The evening comes before the noon,
The scarce risen sun is setting.

While princes hang upon his breath
And nations round are fearing,
Close by his side a daggered death
With sheathless point stands sneering.

That death he took a certain aim,
For Death is stony-hearted
And in the zenith of his fame
Both power and life departed.

Light up thy halls! 'Tis closing day;
I'm drear and lone and far away—
Cold blows on my breast the northwind's bitter sigh,
And oh, my couch is bleak beneath the rainy sky!

Light up thy halls—and think not of me;
That face is absent now, thou hast hated so to see—
Bright be thine eyes, undimmed their dazzling shine,
For never, never more shall they encounter mine!

The desert moor is dark; there is tempest in the air;
I have breathed my only wish in one last, one burning prayer—
A prayer that would come forth, although it lingered long;
That set on fire my heart, but froze upon my tongue.

And now, it shall be done before the morning rise:
I will not watch the sun ascend in yonder skies.
One task alone remains—thy pictured face to view;
And then I got to prove if God, at least, be true!

Do I not see thee now? Thy black resplendent hair;
Thy glory-beaming brow, and smile, how heavenly fair!
Thine eyes are turned away—those eyes I would not see;
Their dark, their deadly ray would more than madden me.

There, go, Deceiver, go! My hand is streaming wet;
My heart's blood flows to buy the blessing—To forget!
Oh could that lost heart give back, back again to thine,
One tenth part of the pain that clouds my dark decline!

Oh could I see thy lids weighed down in cheerless woe;
Too full to hide their tears, too stern to overflow;
Oh could I know thy soul with equal grief was torn,
This fate might be endured—this anguish might be borne!

How gloomy grows the night! 'Tis Gondal's wind that blows;
I shall not tread again the deep glens where it rose—
I feel it on my face—"Where, wild blast, dost thou roam?
What do we, wanderer, here, so far away from home?

"I do not need thy breath to cool my death-cold brow;
But go to that far land, where she is shining now;
Tell Her my latest wish, tell Her my dreary doom;
Say that my pangs are past but Hers are yet to come."

Vain words—vain, frenzied thoughts! No ear can hear me call—
Lost in the vacant air my frantic curses fall—
And could she see me now, perchance her lip would smile,
Would smile in careless pride and utter scorn the while!

And yet for all her hate, each parting glance would tell
A stronger passion breathed, burned, in this last farewell.
Unconquered in my soul the Tyrant rules me still;
Life bows to my control, but Love I cannot kill!

Tell me, watcher, is it winter?
Say how long my sleep has been?
Have the woods I left so lovely
Lost their robes of tender green?

Is the morning slow in coming?
Is the night-time loath to go?
Tell me, are the dreary mountains
Drearier still with drifted snow?

"Captive, since thou sawest the forest,
All its leaves have died away,
And another March has woven
Garlands for another May.

"Ice has barred the Arctic water,
Soft south winds have set it free;
And once more to deep green valley
Golden flowers might welcome thee."

Watcher, in this lonely prison,
Shut from joy and kindly air,
Heaven, descending in a vision,
Taught my soul to do and bear.

It was night, a night in winter;
I lay on the dungeon floor,
And all other sounds were silent—
All, except the river's roar.

Over Death and Desolation,
Fireless hearths and lifeless homes;
Over orphans' heart-sick sorrows,
Over fathers' bloody tombs;

Over friends, that my arms never
Might embrace in love again—
Memory pondered, until madness
Struck its poynaird in my brain.

Deepest slumber followed raving,
Yet, methought, I brooded still;
Still I saw my country bleeding,
Dying for a Tyrant's will—

Not because my bliss was blasted,
Burned within, the avenging flame;
Not because my scattered kindred
Died in woe or lived in shame.

God doth know, I would have given
Every bosom dear to me,
Could that sacrifice have purchased
Tortured Gondal's liberty!

But, that at Ambition's bidding
All her cherished hopes should wane;
That her noblest sons should muster,
Strive and fight, and fall in vain—

Hut and castle, hall and cottage,
Roofless, crumbling to the ground—
Mighty Heaven, a glad Avenger
Thy eternal justice found!

Yes, the arm that once would shudder
Even to pierce a wounded deer,
I beheld it, unrelenting,
Choke in blood it's sovereign's prayer.

Glorious dream! I saw the city
Blazing in imperial shine;
And among adoring thousands
Stood a man of form divine.

None need point the princely victim—
Now he smiles with royal pride!
Now his glance is bright as lightning;
Now—the knife is in his side!

Ha, I saw how death could darken—
Darken that triumphant eye!
His red heart's blood drenched my dagger;
My ear drank his dying sight!

Shadows come! What means this midnight?
O my God, I know it all!
Know the fever-dream is over!
Unavenged the Avengers fall!

"The winter wind is loud and wild;
Come close to me, my darling child!
Forsake thy books and mateless play,
And, while the night is gathering grey,
We'll talk its pensive hours away—

"Ierne, round our sheltered hall,
November's gusts unheeded call;
Not one faint breath can enter here
Enough to wave my daughter's hair;

"And I am glad to watch the blaze
Glance from her eyes, with mimic rays;
To feel her cheek so softly pressed
In happy quiet on my breast;

"But, yet, even this tranquillity
Brings bitter, restless thoughts to me;
And, in the red fire's cheerful glow,
I think of deep glens, blocked with snow;

"I dream of moor, and misty hill,
Where evening closes, dark and chill,
For, lone, among the mountains cold
Lie those that I have loved of old,
And my heart aches, in hopeless pain,
Exhausted with repinings vain,
That I shall greet them ne'er again!"

"Father, in early infancy,
When you were far beyond the sea,
Such thoughts were tyrants over me—
I often sat for hours together,
Through the long nights of angry weather,
Raised on my pillow, to descry
The dim moon struggling in the sky;
Or, with strained ear, to catch the shock
Of rock with wave, and wave with rock.
So would I fearful vigil keep,
And, all for listening, never sleep;
But this world's life has much to dread:
Not so, my father, with the Dead.

"O not for them should we despair;
The grave is drear, but they are not there:
Their dust is mingled with the sod;
Their happy souls are gone to God!
You told me this, and yet you sigh,
And murmur that your friends must die.
Ah, my dear father, tell me why?

"For, if your former words were true,
How useless would such sorrow be!
As wise to mourn the seed which grew
Unnoticed on its parent tree,

"Because it fell in fertile earth
And sprang up to a glorious birth—
Struck deep its root, and lifted high
Its green boughs in the breezy sky!

"But I'll not fear—I will not weep
For those whose bodies rest in sleep:
I know there is a blessed shore
Opening its ports for me and mine;
And, gazing Time's wide waters o'er,
I weary for that land divine,

"Where we were born—where you and I
Shall meet our dearest, when we die;
From suffering and corruption free,
Restored into the Deity."

"Well hast thou spoken, sweet, trustful child!
And wiser than thy sire:
And worldly tempests, raging wild,
Shall strengthen thy desire—

The fervent hope, through storm and foam,
Through wind and Ocean's roar,
To reach, at last, the eternal home—
The steadfast, changeless shore!"

Sacred watcher, wave thy bells!
Fair hill flower and woodland child!
Dear to me in deep green dells—
Dearest on the mountains wild.

Bluebell, even as all divine
I have seen my darling shine—
Bluebell, even as wan and frail
I have seen my darling fail—
Thou hast found a voice for me,
And soothing words are breathed by thee.

Thus they murmur, "Summer's sun
Warms me till my life is done.
Would I rather choose to die
Under winter's ruthless sky?

"Glad I bloom and calm I fade;
Weeping twilight dews my bed;
Mourner, mourner, dry thy tears—
Sorrow comes with lengthened years!"

The battle had passed from the height,
And still did evening fall;
While heaven, with its hosts of night,
Gloriously canopied all.

The dead around were sleeping
On heath and granite grey;
And the dying their last watch were keeping
In the closing of the day.

Awake! awake! how loud the stormy morning
Calls up to life the nations resting round;
Arise! arise! is it the voice of mourning
That breaks our slumber with so wild a sound?

The voice of mourning? Listen to its pealing;
That shout of triumph drowns the sigh of woe.
Each tortured heart forgets its wonted feeling;
Each faded cheek resumes its long-lost glow.

Our souls are full of gladness; God has given
Our arms to victory, our foes to death;
The crimson ensign waves its sheet in heaven,
The sea-green Standard lies in dust beneath.

Patriots, no stain is on your country's glory;
Soldiers, preserve that glory bright and free.
Let Almedore, in peace, and battle gory,
Be still a nobler name for victory.

A sudden chasm of ghastly light
Yawned in the city's reeling wall,
And a long thundering through the night
Proclaimed our triumph—Tyndarum's fall.

The shrieking wind sank mute and mild;
The smothering snow-clouds rolled away;
And cold-how cold!—wan moonlight smiled
Where those black ruins smouldering lay.

'Twas over: All the battle's madness—
The bursting fires, the cannons' roar,
The yells, the groans, the frenzied gladness,
The death, the danger—alarmed no more.

In plundered churches piled with dead
The heavy charger neighed for food;
The wounded soldier laid his head
'Neath roofless chambers splashed with blood.

I could not sleep: through that wild siege
My heart had fiercely burned and bounded;
The outward tumult seemed to assuage
The inward tempest it surrounded.

But dreams like this I cannot bear,
And silence whets the fang of pain;
I felt the full flood of despair
Returning to my breast again.

My couch lay in a ruined Hall,
Whose windows looked on the minster-yard,
Where chill, chill whiteness covered all—
Both stone and urn and withered sward.

The shattered glass let in the air,
And with it came a wandering moan,
A sound unutterably drear
That made me shrink to be alone.

One black yew-tree grew just below—
I thought its boughs so sad might wail;
Their ghostly fingers, flecked with snow,
Rattled against an old vault's rail.

I listened—no; 'twas life that still
Lingered in some deserted heart:
O God! what caused the shuddering shrill,
That anguished, agonizing start?

An undefined, an awful dream
A dream of what had been before;
A memory whose blighting beam
Was flitting o'er me evermore.

A frightful feeling, frenzy born—
I hurried down the dark oak stair;
I reached the door whose hinges torn
Flung streaks of moonshine here and there.

I pondered not; I drew the bar;
An icy glory caught mine eye,
From that wide heaven where every star
Stared like a dying memory;

And there the great Cathedral rose
Discrowned but most majestic so,
It looked down in serene repose
On its own realm of buried woe

All blue and bright, in glorious light,
The morn comes marching on;
And now Zalona's steeples white
Glow golden in the sun.

This day might be a festal day:
The streets are crowded all;
And emerald flags stream broad and gay
From turret, tower, and wall.

And, hark! how music evermore
Is sounding in the sky:
The deep bells boom, the cannon roar,
The trumpets sound on high—

The deep bells boom, the deep bells clash,
Upon the reeling air;
The cannon with unceasing crash
Make answer far and near.

What do those brazen tongues proclaim,
What joyous fete begun?
What offering to our country's fame,
What noble victory won?

Go, ask that solitary sire,
Laid in his house alone,
His silent hearth without a fire
His sons and daughters gone.

Go, ask those children in the street,
Beside their mother's door,
Waiting to hear the lingering feet
That they shall hear no more.

Ask those pale soldiers round the gates,
With famine-kindled eye:
They'll say, "Zalona celebrates
The day that she must die."

The charger, by his manger tied,
Has rested many a day;
Yet, ere the spur have touched his side,
Behold, he sinks away!

And hungry dogs, with wolf-like cry,
Unburied corpses tear,
While their gaunt masters gaze and sigh
And scarce the feast forbear.

Now, look down from Zalona's wall—
There war the unwearied foe;
If ranks before our cannon fall,
New ranks for ever grow.

And many a week, unbroken thus
Their troops our ramparts hem;
And for each man that fights for us,
A hundred fight for them!

Courage and Right and spotless Truth
Were pitched 'gainst trait'rous crime;
We offered all—our age, our youth,
Our brave men in their prime—

And all have failed—the fervent prayers;
The trust in heavenly aid;
Valour and Faith and sealed tears
That would not mourn the dead;

Lips, that did breathe no murmuring word;
Hearts, that did ne'er complain,
Though vengeance held a sheathed sword,
And martyrs bled in vain.

Alas, alas, the Myrtle bowers
By blighting blasts destroyed!
Alas, the Lily's withered flowers
That leave the garden voice!

Unfolds o'er tower, and waves o'er height,
A sheet of crimson sheen:
Is it the setting sun's red light
That stains our standard green?

Heaven help us in this awful hour!
For now might Faith decay—
Now might we doubt God's guardian power
And curse instead of pray.

He will not even let us die—
Not let us die at home;
The foe must see our soldiers fly
As they had feared the tomb;

Because we dare not stay to gain
Those longed-for, glorious graves—
We dare not shrink from slavery's chain
To leave our children slaves!

But when this scene of awful woe
Has neared its final close,
As God forsook our armies, so
May he forsake our foes!

This shall be thy lullaby
Rocking on the stormy sea,
Though it roar in thunder wild
Sleep, stilly sleep, my dark haired child.

When our shuddering boat was crossing
Elderno lake so rudely tossing
Then 'twas first my nursling smiled;
Sleep, softly sleep, my fair-browed child.

Waves above thy cradle break.
Foamy tears are on thy cheek
Yet the Ocean's self grows mild
When it bears my slumbering child.

"Listen! when your hair, like mine,
Takes a tint of silver grey;
When your eyes, with dimmer shine,
Watch life's bubbles float away;

"When you, young man, have borne like me,
The weary weight of sixty-three,
Then shall penance sore be paid
For these hours so wildly squandered;
And the words that now fall dead
On your ears, be deeply pondered;
Pondered and approved at last,
But their virtue will be past!

"Glorious is the prize of Duty,
Though she be a serious power;
Treacherous all the lures of Beauty,
Thorny bud and poisonous flower!

"Mirth is but a mad beguiling
Of the golden-gifted Time;
Love, a demon-meteor, wiling
Heedless feet to gulfs of crime.

"Those who follow earthly pleasure,
Heavenly knowledge will not lead;
Wisdom hides from them her treasure,
Virtue bids them evil-speed!

"Vainly may their hearts, repenting,
Seek for aid in future years;
Wisdom scorned knows no relenting;
Virtue is not won by tears.

"Fain would we your steps reclaim,
Waken fear and holy shame.
And to this end, our council well
And kindly doomed you to a cell
Whose darkness may, perchance, disclose
A beacon-guide from sterner woes."

So spake my judge—then seized his lamp
And left me in the dungeon damp,
A vault like place whose stagnant air
Suggests and nourishes despair!

Rosina, this had never been
Except for you, my despot queen!
Except for you the billowy sea
Would now be tossing under me,
The wind's wild voice my bosom thrill
And my glad heart bound wilder still,

Flying before the rapid gale
Those wondrous southern isles to hail
Which wait for my companions free
But thank your passion—not for me!

You know too well—and so do I—
Your haughty beauty's sovereignty;
Yet have I read those falcon eyes—
Have dived in their mysteries—
Have studied long their glance and feel
It is not love those eyes reveal.

They Flash, they burn with lightning shine,
But not with such fond fire as mine;
The tender star fades faint and wan
Before Ambition's scorching sun.
So deem I now—and Time will prove
If I have wronged Rosina's love.

Cold in the earth, and the deep snow piled above thee!
Far, far removed, cold in the dreary grave!
Have I forgot, my Only Love, to love thee,
Severed at last by Time's all-severing wave?

Now, when alone, do my thoughts no longer hover
Over the mountains on that northern shore;
Resting their wings where heath and fern-leaves cover
Thy noble heart for ever, ever more?

Cold in the earth, and fifteen wild Decembers
From those brown hills have melted into spring—
Faithful indeed in the spirit that remembers
After such years of change and suffering!

Sweet Love of youth, forgive if I forget thee
While the World's tide is bearing me along:
Other desires and other hopes beset me,
Hopes which obscure but cannot do thee wrong.

No later light has lightened up my heaven;
No second morn has ever shone for me:
All my life's bliss from thy dear life was given—
All my life's bliss is in the grave with thee.

But when the days of golden dreams had perished
And even Despair was powerless to destroy,
Then did I learn how existence could be cherished,
Strengthened and fed without the aid of joy;

Then did I check the tears of useless passion,
Weaned my young soul from yearning after thine;
Sternly denied its burning wish to hasten
Down to that tomb already more than mine!

And even yet, I dare not let it languish,
Dare not indulge in Memory's rapturous pain;
Once drinking deep of that divinest anguish,
How come I seek the empty world again.

There swept adown that dreary glen
A wilder sound than mountain wind:
The thrilling shouts of fighting men
With something sadder far behind.

The thrilling shouts they died away
Before the night came greyly down;
But closed not with the closing day
The choking sob, the tortured moan.

Down in a hollow, sunk in shade,
Where dark heath waved in secret gloom,
A weary bleeding form was laid,
Waiting the death that was to come.

"Well, some may hate, and some may scorn,
And some may quite forget thy name,
But my said heart must ever mourn
Thy ruined hopes, thy blighted fame."

'Twas thus I thought, an hour ago,
Even weeping o'er that wretch's woe.
One word turned back my gushing tears,
And lit my altered eye with sneers.

"Then bless the friendly dust," I said,
"That hides thy unlamented head.
Vain as thou wert, and weak as vain,
The slave of falsehood, pride and pain,
My heart has nought akin to thine—
Thy soul is powerless over mine."

But these were thoughts that vanished too—
Unwise, unholy, and untrue—
Do I despise the timid deer
Because his limbs are fleet with fear?

Or would I mock the wolf's death-howl
Because his form is gaunt and foul?
Or hear with joy the leveret's cry
Because it cannot bravely die?

No! Then above his memory
Let pity's heart as tender be:
Say, "Earth lie lightly on that breast,
And, kind Heaven, grant that spirit rest!"

Why ask to know the date—the clime?
More than mere words they cannot be:
Men knelt to God and worshipped crime,
And crushed the helpless, even as we.

But they had learnt, from length of strife
Of civil war and anarchy,
To laugh at death and look on life
With somewhat lighter sympathy.

It was the autumn of the year,
The time to labouring peasants dear;
Week after week, from noon to noon,
September shone as bright as June—

Still, never hand a sickle held;
The crops were garnered in the field—
Trod out and ground by horses' feet
While every ear was milky sweet;
And kneaded on the threshing-floor
With mire of tears and human gore.
Some said they thought that heaven's pure rain
Would hardly bless those fields again:
Not so—the all-benignant skies
Rebuked that fear of famished eyes—
July passed on with showers and dew,
And August glowed in showerless blue;
No harvest time could be more fair
Had harvest fruits but ripened there.

And I confess that hate of rest,
And thirst for things abandoned now,
Had weaned me from my country's breast
And brought me to that land of woe.

Enthusiast—in a name delighting,
My alien sword I drew to free
One race, beneath two standards, fighting
For Loyalty and Liberty—

When kindred strive—God help the weak!
A brother's ruth 'tis vain to seek:
At first, it hurt my chivalry
To join them in their cruelty;
But I grew hard—I learnt to wear
An iron front to terror's prayer;
I learnt to turn my ears away
From torture's groans, as well as they.

By force I learnt—What power had I
To say the conquered should not die?
What heart, one trembling foe to save
When hundreds daily filled the grave?
Yet, there were faces that could move
A moment's flash of human love;
And there were fates that made me feel
I was not, to the centre, steel—
I've often witnessed wise men fear
To meet distress which they foresaw;
And seeming cowards nobly bear
A doom that thrilled the brave with awe.

Strange proofs I've seen, how hearts could hide
Their secret with a life-long pride,
And then reveal it as they died—
Strange courage, and strange weakness too,
In that last hour when most are true,
And timid natures strangely nerved
To deeds from which the desperate swerved.
These I may tell; but, leave them now:
Go with me where my thoughts would go;
Now all today and all last night
I've had one scene before my sight—

Wood-shadowed dales, a harvest moon
Unclouded in its glorious noon;
A solemn landscape wide and still;
A red fire on a distant hill—
A line of fires, and deep below
Another dusker, drearier glow—
Charred beams, and lime, and blackened stones
Self-piled in cairns o'er burning bones,
And lurid flames that licked the wood,
Then quenched their glare in pools of blood.

But yester-eve—No! never care;
Let street and suburb smoulder there—
Smoke-hidden in the winding glen
They lay too far to vex my ken.

Four score shot down—all veterans strong;
One prisoner spared: their leader—young,
And he within his house was laid
Wounded and weak and nearly dead.
We gave him life against his will,
For he entreated us to kill—
But statue-like we saw his tears—
And harshly fell our captain's sneers:

"Now, heaven forbid!" with scorn he said,
"That noble gore our hands should shed
Like common blood—retain thy breath,
Or scheme if thou canst purchase death.
When men are poor we sometimes hear
And pitying grant that dastard prayer;
When men are rich we make them buy
The pleasant privilege to die.
O, we have castles reared for kings,
Embattled towers and buttressed wings
Thrice three feet thick and guarded well
With chain and bolt and sentinel!

We build our despots' dwellings sure
Knowing they love to live secure—
And our respect for royalty
Extends to thy estate and thee!"

The suppliant groaned; his moistened eye
Swam wild and dim with agony.
The gentle blood could ill sustain
Degrading taunts, unhonoured pain.

Bold had he shown himself to lead;
Eager to smite and proud to bleed;
A man amid the battle's storm:
An infant in the after calm.
Beyond the town his mansion stood
Girt round with pasture land and wood;
And there our wounded soldiers lying
Enjoyed the ease of wealth in dying.

For him, no mortal more than he
Had softened life with luxury;
And truly did our priest declare
"Of good things he had had his share."

We lodged him in an empty place,
The full moon beaming on his face
Through shivered glass and ruins made
Where shell and ball the fiercest played.

I watched his ghastly couch beside
Regardless if he lived or died—
Nay, muttering curses on the breast
Whose ceaseless moans denied me rest.

"Twas hard, I know, 'twas harsh to say
"Hell snatch thy worthless soul away!"
But then 'twas hard my lids to keep
Through the long night estranged from sleep.
Captive and keeper both outworn
Each in his misery yearned for morn,
Even though returning morn should bring
Intenser toil and suffering.

Slow, slow it came! Our dreary room
Grew drearier with departing gloom;
Yet as the west wind warmly blew
I felt my pulses bound anew,
And turned to him—Nor breeze, nor ray
Revived that mould of shattered clay.
Scarce conscious of his pain he lay—
Scarce conscious that my hands removed
The glittering toys high lightness loved—
The jewelled rings and locket fair
Where rival curls of silken hair
Sable and brown revealed to me
A tale of doubtful constancy.

"Forsake the world without regret,"
I murmured in contemptuous tone;
"The world poor wretch will soon forget
Thy noble name when thou art gone!
Happy, if years of slothful shame
Could perish like a noble name—
If God did no account require
And being with breathing might expire!"
And words of such contempt I said,
Harsh insults o'er a dying bed,
Which as they darken memory now
Disturb my pulse and flush my brow.
I know that Justice holds in store
Reprisals for those days of gore;
Not for the blood but for the sin
Of stifling mercy's voice within.

The blood spilt gives no pang at all;
It is my conscience haunting me,
Telling how oft my lips shed gall
On many a thing too weak to be,
Even in thought, my enemy;
And whispering ever, when I pray,
"God will repay—God will repay!"

He does repay and soon and well
The deeds that turn his earth to hell,
The wrongs that aim a venomed dart
Through nature at the Eternal Heart.

Surely my cruel tongue was cursed
I know my prisoner heard me speak
A transient gleam of feeling burst
And wandered o'er his haggard cheek
And from his quivering lids there stole
A look to melt a demon's soul
A silent prayer more powerful far
Than any breathed petitions are
Pleading in mortal agony
To mercy's Source but not to me.
Now I recall that glance and groan
And wring my hands in vain distress;
Then I was adamantine stone
Nor felt one touch of tenderness.

My plunder ta'em I left him there
Without one breath of morning air
To struggle with his last despair,
Regardless of the 'wildered cry
Which wailed for death, yea wailed to die.

I left him there unwatched, alone,
And eager sought the court below
Where o'er a trough of chiselled stone
An ice cold well did gurgling flow.
The water in its basin shed
A stranger tinge of fiery red.
I drank and scarcely marked the hue;
My food was dyed with crimson too.
As I went out, a ragged child
With wasted cheek and ringlets wild,
A shape of fear and misery,
Raised up her helpless hands to me
And begged her father's face to see.
I spurned the piteous wretch away:

"Thy father's face is lifeless clay
As thine mayst be ere fall of day
Unless the truth be quickly told—
Where they have hid thy father's gold."
Yet in the intervals of pain
He heard my taunts and moaned again
And mocking moans did I reply
And asked him why he would not die
In noble agony—uncomplaining.
Was it not foul disgrace and shame
To thus disgrace his ancient name?

Just then a comrade hurried in
"Alas," he cried, "sin genders sin
For every soldier slain they've sworn
To hang up five tomorrow morn.
They've ta'en of stragglers sixty-three,
Full thirty from one company,
And all my father's family;

And comrade thou hadst only one—
They've ta'en thy all, thy little son."
Down at my captive's feet I fell
I had no option in despair
"As thou wouldst save thy soul from hell
My heart's own darling bid them spare
Or human hate and hate divine
Blight every orphan flower of thine."

He raised his head—from death beguiled,
He wakened up—he almost smiled,
"I lost last night my only child
Twice in my arms twice on my knee
You stabbed my child and laughed at me
And so," with choking voice he said,
"I trust in God I hope she's dead
Yet not to thee, not even to thee
Would I return such misery.
Such is that fearful grief I know
I will not cause thee equal woe
Write that they harm no infant there
Write that it is my latest prayer."
I wrote—he signed—and thus did save
My treasure from the gory grave
And O! My soul longed wildly then
To give his saviour life again.
But heedless of my gratitude
The silent corpse before me lay
And still methinks in gloomy mood
I see it fresh as yesterday
The sad face raised imploringly
To mercy's God and not to me.

I could not rescue him; his child
I found alive, and tended well
But she was full of anguish wild
And hated me like we hate hell
And weary with her savage woe
One moon-less night I let her go.

How do I love on summer nights
To sit within this Norman door,
Whose sombre portal hides the lights
Thickening above me evermore!

How do I love to hear the flow
Of Aspin's water murmuring low;
And hours long listen to the breeze
That sighs in Rockden's waving trees.

Tonight, there is no wind to wake
One ripple on the lonely lake;
Tonight, the clouds subdued and grey
Starlight and moonlight shut away.

'Tis calm and still and almost drear,
So utter is the solitude;
But still I love to linger here
And form my mood to nature's mood.

There's a wild walk beneath the rocks
Following the bend of Aspin's side;
'Tis worn by feet of mountain-flocks
That wander down to drink the tide.

Never by cliff and gnarled tree
Wound fairy path so sweet to me;
Yet of the native shepherds none,
In open day and cheerful sun,
Will tread its labyrinths alone;
Far less when evening's pensive hour
Hushes the bird and shuts the flower,
And gives to Fancy magic power
O'er each familiar tone.

For round their hearths they'll tell the tale,
And every listener swears it's true,
How wanders there a phantom pale
With spirit-eyes of dreamy blue.

It always walks with head decline,
Its long curls move in the wind,
Its face is fair — divinely fair;
But brooding on that angel brow
Rests such a shade of deep despair
As nought divine could ever know.

How oft in twilight, lingering lone,
I've stood to watch that phantom rise,
And seen in mist and moonlit stone
Its gleaming hair and solemn eyes.

The ancient men, in secret, say
'Tis the first chief of Aspin grey
That haunts his feudal home;
But why, around that alien grave
Three thousand miles beyond the wave,
Where his exiled ashes lie
Under the cape of England's sky,
Doth he not rather roam?

I've seen his picture in the hall;
It hangs upon an eastern wall,
And often when the sun declines
That picture like an angel shines;
And when the moonbeam, chill and blue,
Streams the spectral windows through,
That picture's like a spectre too.

The hall is full of portraits rare;
Beauty and mystery mingle there:
At his right hand an infant fair
Looks from its golden frame;
And just like his its ringlets bright,
Its large dark eyes of shadowy light,
Its cheeks pure hue, its forehead white,
And like its noble name.

Daughter divine! and could his gaze,
Fall coldly on thy peerless face?
And did he never smile to see
Himself restored to infancy?

Never part back that golden flow
Of curls, and kiss that pearly brow,
And feel no other earthly bliss
Was equal to that parent's kiss?

No; turn towards the western side;
There stands Sidonia's deity,
In all her glory, all her pride!
And truly like a god she seems:
Some god of wild enthusiast's dreams;
And this is she for whom he died:
For whom his spirit, unforgiven,
Wanders unsheltered, shut from heaven —
An outcast for eternity.

Those eyes are dust, those lips are clay;
That form is mouldered all away;
Nor thought, nor sense, nor pulse, nor breath:
The whole devoured and lost in death!

There is no worm, however mean,
That, living, is not nobler now
Than she, Lord Alfred's idol queen,
So loved, so worshipped, long ago.

O come away! the Norman door
Is silvered with a sudden shine;
Come, leave these dreams o'er things of yore
And turn to Nature's face divine.

O'er wood and wold, o'er flood and fell,
O'er flashing lake and gleaming dell,
The harvest moon looks down;
And when heaven smiles with love and light,
And earth looks back so dazzling bright —
In such a scene, on such a night,
Earth's children should not frown.

The evening sun was sinking down
On low green hills and clustered trees;
It was a scene as fair and lone
As ever felt the soothing breeze
That bends the grass, when day is gone,
And gives the wave a brighter blue,
And makes the soft white clouds sail on
Like spirits of ethereal dew.
Which all the morn had hovered o'er
The azure flowers where they were nursed,
And now return to heaven once more
Where their bright glories shone at first.

INDEX TO FIRST LINES